the little book of
living small

the little book of
living small

Laura Fenton | **Photographs by Weston Wells**

GIBBS SMITH
TO ENRICH AND INSPIRE HUMANKIND

First Edition
24 23 22 21   5 4

Text © 2020 Laura Fenton
Photographs © 2020 Weston Wells
except page 5 by Natalia Lorca Ruiz, courtesy of Atelier Armbruster,
Page 166, lower right, courtesy of Artek,
Page 177, upper right, courtesy of IKEA; lower left, courtesy of Ouef,
Page 186, by Francesco Bertocci, courtesy of Atelier Armbruster,
Page 193, upper right by Leslie Santarina, courtesy of Crystal Palecek; lower, courtesy of Vitsoe

Published by
Gibbs Smith
P.O. Box 667
Layton, Utah 84041

1.800.835.4993 orders
www.gibbs-smith.com

Designed by Debbie Berne
Printed and bound in China

Gibbs Smith books are printed on either recycled, 100% post-consumer waste, FSC-certified papers or on paper produced from sustainable PEFC-certified forest/controlled wood source. Learn more at www.pefc.org.

Library of Congress Cataloging-in-Publication Data
Names: Fenton, Laura, 1980- author. | Wells, Weston, illustrator.
Title: The little book of living small / Laura Fenton ; photographs by Weston Wells.
Description: First edition. | Layton, Utah : Gibbs Smith, [2020] | Summary: "Small-space secrets and real-life solutions for living in 1,200 square feet or less. Highly readable with actionable advice and beautiful interior photography, this book is one that readers can refer back to often when they need a boost of inspiration or motivation."— Provided by publisher.
Identifiers: LCCN 2019023462 | ISBN 9781423652533 (hardcover) | ISBN 9781423652540 (epub)
Subjects: LCSH: Small houses. | Apartments.
Classification: LCC NA7533 .F46 2020 | DDC 728/.1—dc23
LC record available at https://lccn.loc.gov/2019023462

To our son, William, the biggest, little thing to ever come into our world.

contents

foreword

"I have never been forced to accept compromises but I have willingly accepted constraints."

CHARLES EAMES

When I started out life in New York City, my apartment was 250 square feet of heaven. It was my first home as an adult: I lived there for more than fifteen years, and our daughter lived there until she was one. That home gave me a life in the city that I could never have afforded. It also gave me a neighborhood—the West Village—and neighbors who changed my life and became the bedrock of my experience in the city.

There is nothing like living a cozy life amongst people you feel a kinship with. That home helped support a truly *big* life. That home also taught me a lot about how to change and shift space to make it meet my changing needs.

As with Charles Eames's great quote above, I realized a number of times that moving to a bigger space would not solve my problems. The constraints of a smaller space in a neighborhood and building I loved forced me to keep seeking solutions and redoing my small home in ways that amazed even me.

I learned how to work with paint, lighting, closets, and doors (remove them!). I learned how to build my own solutions when I couldn't buy them, and I learned all of the ingredients that allow us to have that wonderful feeling of being comfortable at home. Surprisingly, space was—for many years—the least

of my issues; I saw it as a constraint and never as a compromise.

I started Apartment Therapy as a service in 2001 (I worked with people in their homes) and the website ApartmentTherapy.com in 2004, because I was living what felt like an amazing experiment that was worth sharing. I also started the business because I was inspired by the "simple movement" of the early 2000s. Being from a generation that reacted to the excesses of American cities and wanted more from life, not more things, home became the very real center of building a life that I could truly believe in and that would get me out of bed each morning with excitement.

Not only is this still true, but, I will also admit, that this past summer I had my first experience of wanting to move *out* of a home that felt big and uncomfortable. After four years in a Brooklyn brownstone, which seemed so lovely and roomy at first, my daughter and I both decided it was simply too much space. We are now happily living in a two bedroom, which is far smaller—and we couldn't be more comfortable.

Best,
Maxwell Ryan
Founder of Apartment Therapy Media

introduction

It's a small world. Tiny houses, minimalism, and a less-is-more attitude are everywhere today. After years of a "bigger is better" mentality toward homes, people are realizing that extra square footage does not equal greater happiness.

A generation ago, the ideas that a smaller home might be better and that quality should come before quantity were revolutionary. Today, there are four different television shows about tiny houses and more than a million images with the hashtags #tinyhouse and #tinyhome on Instagram. For the first time in decades, the average house size in the United States is shrinking. (The all-time high of 2,467 square feet in 2015 was 49 percent bigger than in 1978!) In recent years, megacatalog retailers have introduced collections of small-scale furniture to cater to a growing market, and a "Want Better Not More" poster has become a cult best seller. Small is suddenly a *big* deal.

Smaller homes are trending for a number of reasons: More than a decade after the housing crisis, builders are finally building houses for regular people, not just the rich. Millennials, who have witnessed the dangers of overextending, are seeking out more affordable housing options and delaying home purchases. And those same younger people are moving to cities in increasing numbers.

Choosing small is not just a financial decision or a reaction to the housing market. It is also an ecological choice for an increasingly green-minded sector of homeowners. The same energy that has people across the globe protesting in demand of climate change action has people reconsidering how and where they ought to live.

The small home trend is also closely related to the minimalism movement that turned Marie Kondo into a household name. Indeed, the goal of living small is to streamline every part of our lives.

But the road to tiny is not as simple as deciding to downsize your home. Choosing small is a lifestyle that impacts every part of one's life—not just the four walls that surround us. A smaller-than-average home requires dedication and discipline, but it rewards its inhabitants with greater freedom.

This book is a comprehensive guide to the "small" lifestyle. It will show you how to make the most of limited square footage—with grace and style. It will also help you discover the joy of living well with less in all aspects of your life. A small home can provide the same material and spiritual comforts as a mansion—whether you are a single person or a family with kids. This book explores both the motivation behind choosing to live small, as well as the practical, everyday advice for managing a tight footprint.

I know about living small from first-hand experience. I've lived in New York City for more than twenty years, and as a mother and wife, I know what it's like to share a small space. I'm also a journalist. I have spent my career writing about homes and how people live, so

I've had an inside look into how others make their small spaces work. When *Parents* magazine, where I am the lifestyle director, published a story on families living in small spaces in 2017, it quickly became one of the most popular home decorating stories we've run, which was one of my first clues that I needed to write this book.

As a city dweller, I have lived in a series of impossibly small spaces, including an AC-less university dorm room shared by three girls, a 6' x 8' bedroom in an apartment with no living room, and a teeny-tiny studio that was made livable by a Murphy bed.

Today I live in less than seven hundred square feet with my husband and son. Our friends may have grander spaces, but I don't think they are happier for it. In fact, I suspect we may have the better deal: My family lives in the city we love, but we have less stress with our lower mortgage payments. Our renovations were relatively cheap because our space is small. We have less clutter in our lives and our son has fewer toys for us to pick up. Our kitchen is a model of efficiency. Our wardrobes are edited down to things we love. If my husband and I stay for the long haul, we have a place that will feel quite spacious when our son moves out. And we have peace of mind knowing we're living lightly on the earth. We're living our best lives in less than 230 square feet per person.

"It is in the everyday things around us that the beauty of life lies."
LAURA INGALLS WILDER

I believe any space can be made to work better and harder. Our home had an efficient layout, but we also carefully planned and calculated the ways to make our home work for us—and we've adapted when our needs have changed. You can do the same with your home.

In this book, I will share with you what I have learned over almost two decades living in small spaces, interviewing other tiny home inhabitants, researching the topic, and writing about it all. I also hope I'll inspire you to embrace your own small-space journey and discover the freedom that living small provides. Welcome to your new small life.

YOUR LITTLE BOOK OF LIVING SMALL

This book is meant to be both a dream book and an instruction manual. I hope the pictures will inspire you and that the words will inform you. My publisher and I chose to make this book small in size because we wanted you to pick it up and read it—maybe not cover to cover, but this book is not intended to be just a coffee table showpiece—it's meant to be dog-eared and underlined. I hope it becomes a resource you will refer to often.

While you can choose your definition of *small*, I set my own rules for what to include in this book. So often, books and magazine articles about small spaces show homes that are neither small nor places where people live full-time (something that has always frustrated me!). For *The Little Book of Living Small* I have chosen to feature only primary residences—no weekend houses, pieds-à-terre, or AirBnBs. I also chose to limit the size of the homes to roughly less than four hundred square feet for a single person, less than seven hundred square feet for a couple, and less than three hundred square feet per person for a family of three or more. (City dwellers, I know you may be thinking nine hundred square feet sounds like a huge apartment for three people but finding houses of less than one thousand square feet is rare!) The smallest home featured in this book is 248 square feet, and the largest homes are 1,200 square feet.

I hope seeing these homes will help you envision your own life with less. When *Dwell* magazine featured a tiny two-bedroom owned by designer Jacqueline Schmidt in 2014, the photos opened my eyes to what kind of space my family could live in. Seeing her home gave me the courage to say yes to buying a one-bedroom apartment while pregnant, knowing that our dining alcove could become a second "bedroom" with the addition of sliding doors. (You can find Jacqueline's home on page 83 and mine on page 145 to see how her space inspired mine.)

For this book, we also chose to shoot the case study homes as they are. We didn't bring in a team of stylists and vanloads of props to make these spaces into stylized vignettes. Instead, my photographer husband and I came to each home with some fresh flowers and open minds. The photographs of the houses and apartments you see are how the homes these people live in look every day. This may not sound like such a big deal, but after nearly two decades in the magazine industry I can tell you it is not the norm.

All of this is to say, I have tried to create a different kind of book: one that shows you honestly how people are living. I hope it will inspire you and maybe even change the way you live.

WHAT IS LIVING SMALL?

Tiny. Little. Petite. Diminutive. Mini. There are dozens of ways to describe a small space. *Merriam-Webster* gives the primary definition of "small" as "having comparatively little size or slight dimensions." *Comparatively* is the key word here. My idea of small may vary greatly from yours. For some, two thousand square feet may feel tight after living in twice that space. In my early twenties, my friends were astounded that I could live in a 250-square-foot studio but compared to the county park cabin I had recently shared, it was my own personal palace. Small is relative and your idea of small may change over time. But no matter how many square feet you inhabit:

Living small is simple.
Living small is smart.
Living small is responsible.

When it comes to lifestyle, there are some definitions of the word that "small" is not. Small-space living is not cramped, paltry, inadequate, or of little consequence. Small is less, but better. Living small is choosing quality over quantity and experiences over things.

"Be content with what you have; rejoice in the way things are. When you realize there is nothing lacking, the whole world belongs to you."

LAO TZU

WHO IS LIVING SMALL FOR?

Anyone at any stage of life can choose to live small—or find themselves doing so, unexpectedly.

- This book is for the student navigating how to set up her first home away from home.

- It's for the recent grads sharing a tiny apartment.

- It's for the young couple moving in together and fitting two lives into a space that once held one.

- It's for the family of three that is trying to make their one-bedroom work for one more year while they save up for a bigger place.

- It's for the family who decides they'd rather have experiences than a rambling house.

- It's for the city-dwelling clan who decides to stay put—even when space gets tight.

- It's for the newly minted empty nesters ready to downsize from the home in which they raised their children.

- It's for the retiree longing for a more manageable space.

This book is for *you*.

WHY GO SMALL?

For many, living in a small space is not a choice, but a necessity. But for those who could choose to live large, there are many reasons to limit your footprint—from economical to philosophical. No matter what your circumstances, there are advantages to living small:

A small home will cost less—both to buy or rent *and* to keep up.

A small home is easier to maintain. Less space means less to clean; fewer belongings mean less to keep tidy and organized.

A small home is better for the earth. We use less energy to heat, cool, and power smaller homes. We also take up fewer resources to furnish and maintain them.

A small home forces simplicity. With less space to squirrel away our belongings, we can live with the things we truly love and use.

A small home fosters closeness. Families and couples living in tighter quarters spend more time in each other's presence, allowing for more moments of intimacy.

"I believe we intuitively desire simpler lives filled with high-quality experiences, relationships, and possessions."

GRAHAM HILL, FOUNDER OF TREEHUGGER

These advantages will manifest themselves in all parts of your life. Choosing to live small will mean you have:

Less stress. You'll worry less about the cost and work of keeping up a larger home.

More time. Fewer hours spent cleaning and maintaining your home means more time doing the things you love.

More money. Spending less on your home means you'll have more to save and spend. You can chip away at debt faster, retire sooner, or travel more.

More meaning. Freed of things you do not need or want, your home will be cozier and imbued with substance.

IT'S A SMALL WORLD

Saving money, saving time—these are admirable ambitions, but what about saving the world? That may sound like a tall order, but choosing to live in less space, is one of the most basic things you can do to reduce your carbon footprint. And it is one of the reasons I am so passionate about living small.

You don't need to go off the grid in a self-sufficient tiny house to live small in an ecological sense. City living, for example, is one of the most sustainable and resource- and energy-efficient lifestyles. By some estimates, households in the inner city consume 70 percent less energy than those living within suburban sprawl or out in the country. Living in an urban area reduces your carbon footprint because city dwellers rarely drive to work, to get groceries, or to take their children to school. Homes with shared walls and apartments stacked on top of each other lose much less heat than stand-alone dwellings. My hometown of New York City is the most energy- and resource-efficient place in the United States on a per-capita basis.

No matter where you live, heating and air conditioning account for the majority of an individual's home energy usage. Once you downsize your square footage you immediately have less to heat and cool, thereby reducing your drain on our Earth's resources. Likewise, if you are renovating or building a small space from scratch, you'll use fewer materials to create your space. Smaller homes are clearly the more sustainable choice. Who knows? Maybe in a few years building increasingly large houses will be considered totally irresponsible, in the same way driving a Hummer seems today.

However, you don't have to wait for the rest of the world to figure out that living small is the most sustainable choice. Go greener today: take your ethos of living small and apply it to all aspects of your home.

"Never doubt that a small group of thoughtful, committed citizens can change the world; indeed, it's the only thing that ever has."
MARGARET MEAD

the small space commandments

Your small space can be a white-walled shrine to minimalism or a cozy den of personal treasures. Whatever your style of space, I do have a few firmly held beliefs—commandments, if you will—that apply to every small space.

1. You shall honor the space you have.
Show respect and remain grateful for what you have—even if it's not much—and treat your home like a place that you value.

2. You shall not covet bigger houses.
Yes, you can keep your Pinterest "Dream Houses" board, but don't long for more than you need. Try dreaming about the ideal tiny home instead.

3. You shall live with what you love.
Edit the objects in your home so that only those that are useful or adored (ideally both) remain.

4. You shall not hoard.
We are blessed to live in a time of abundance. Don't hang on to things you *might* use one day. Pass them on to someone in need.

5. You shall use resources wisely.
Living small is one way to reduce your environmental impact, but it doesn't give you a free pass to blast the AC, skip the recycling and composting, or drive a gas guzzler.

6. You shall value quality over quantity.
"Want better, not more" are words to live by in any walk of life, but especially in a small space in which your possessions are edited down to a minimum.

7. You shall not have off-site storage space.
The answer to your home's clutter woes is not an auxiliary space that is hard to access and expensive to maintain. (See page 205.)

8. You shall buy only what you need.
Technology has made it easier than ever to borrow many of the things that we use infrequently, from books to power tools to camping gear.

9. You shall tidy and organize daily.
A house does not keep itself: the secret to a happy home is for everything to have a place and to do the work to put those things back in their places.

10. You shall cherish your home.
Protect and care for the home you have. The satisfaction you'll feel when you do will reward you daily.

case studies

Take a look inside a dozen little homes, from a not-so-tiny
tiny house in the Rockies to a gut-renovated two-bedroom apartment in
New York City. These homes are full of smart ideas
for how to live well in a small space.

The dining nook's built-in banquette has storage beneath the cushioned seats: a space for linens on the left and filing drawers on the right. The window above the dining area lets light into the bathroom beyond.

the ship-shape suite

Manhattan, New York | Square Feet: 355

When Alisa Regas bought her studio apartment nearly twenty years ago, she wasn't the least bit worried about its size. Before the advent of tell-all renovation blogs, Alisa had clipped space-saving ideas from magazines and books for years and had even tracked down architects to ask them for their sources. For her own renovation, she hired architect Kenny Payero, who helped Alisa to reimagine the 355 square feet into a one-bedroom, complete with a dining space and even a dressing "room." Alisa also brought in an interior designer, Mark Enos, to help with the furnishing choices and layout. The collaborative effort resulted in a space that is as efficient as a ship's cabin, but just as stylish as a luxe Tribeca loft.

The apartment began to feel small when John, Alisa's boyfriend (now husband), came into the picture. In an only-in-New York story, a second equally tiny studio in the building became available, and the couple snapped it up—even though it did not adjoin the original apartment. The extra space, referred to as "the parlor," is used for entertaining and for visiting guests. Alisa is a performing arts producer, so she also lends the space to artists who have made the parlor their New York base while working on new projects. These pages show the original studio, which is where Alisa and John live their daily lives. It remains almost completely unchanged from her initial renovation twenty years ago—proof of its timeless design.

◁◁ By opening up the walls, the architect found space to build in corner shelves and a nook that holds wine bottles.

◁ An all-white palette and a minimalist glass enclosure help make the bathroom feel spacious. Demolition revealed space behind the original medicine cabinet and Alisa's architect designed a new one that is a full foot deep.

◁ The metal front door acts as a memo board. By opting for a now-discontinued eighteen-inch-wide refrigerator, Alisa was also able to fit in a tiny pantry cabinet that keeps her small kitchen from getting overwhelmed with clutter.

▷ In Alisa's kitchen, almost everything is miniature: the sink measures twenty inches, the dishwasher eighteen inches, and the range twenty inches. Because the space is small, Alisa could afford custom cabinetry, cherrywood counters, and high-end faucets and fixtures.

A custom floor-to-ceiling bookcase holds all of Alisa's books and doubles as a bedside table.

△   Built-in dressers separate the bed from the dressing area.

▷   One of the closet doors unfolds to become a bifold mirror.

◁◁   Carefully chosen furnishings give the small living room the feel of a grander space. Leaving the windows bare (Alisa lives on an upper floor on the garden side of her building) also expands the feeling of the room.

▽   With doors on two sides of the bedroom, Alisa was left with just a small stretch of wall that necessitated a custom sofa to fit the space.

"The essence of interior design will always be about people and how they live."

ALBERT HADLEY

A botanical wallpaper from Chasing Paper adds a punch of style to the apartment from the moment you enter through the door. A slender bench and a few hooks make the transition from the outside easier and put what might otherwise be unused space to work.

the decorator special

Manhattan, New York | Square Feet: 750

When Crystal and Taylor Nielsen decided to move their family from Salt Lake City to Manhattan when a job opportunity came up for Taylor, the couple had already downsized from a six-bedroom home to a four-bedroom a few years earlier. Moving to New York City, they knew they'd be downsizing further, so when the buyer for their Utah home offered to buy it furnished, the Nielsens said yes, and came with only their clothes, personal belongings, and some kitchen gear.

Crystal and Taylor decided location and light were more important than extra space and settled on a one-bedroom apartment just two blocks from the subway on the Upper West Side. Trained as an interior designer, Crystal was confident she could make the apartment work for their family of four. She used her designer's eye to purchase just the right things for their new smaller space which was an essentially blank slate.

What is most impressive about Crystal's transformation is that she did nothing to the space that could not be undone at the end of their lease. A Murphy bed and a bunk bed give the family extra space without any structural interventions. Peel-and-stick wallpaper in the entryway, adhesive floor stickers in the kitchen, and updated light fixtures can all be easily removed on moving day.

Crystal's other secret weapon was generous storage space: the apartment had only one bedroom, but it had five closets, all of which Crystal tricked out with off-the-shelf organizers. Because the family can tuck away all of their clothes in closets, they can do without a single dresser. A dedicated pantry/utility closet makes the microscopic kitchen work too.

Now that they've spent two years living in the big city with young kids and realize how freeing it is to live with less, the couple is dreaming of other cities they may move to next.

"Forget the floor plans. Arrange
the furniture where it is the most
comfortable and will look best."

ALBERT HADLEY

◁ The main living space is home to the dining room, living room, music room, and by night, the parents' bedroom. Painting one section of the wall a dark navy color and using the sofa to divide the room helped Crystal delineate the specific spaces within the room.

▽ Taylor got the piano for Crystal as a surprise. He knew she wanted one and realized it was possible to fit one in their home even though the space was limited.

▽   This kitchen is tiny at 6' x 6', but it's got a dishwasher, a four-burner stove, and a full-size fridge. Crystal added extra storage by installing two shelves, which hold some of the family's dishes and serving pieces. To freshen up the look, Crystal purchased vinyl floor stickers from Etsy. She also swapped out the cabinet hardware and overhead light fixture.

▷   Tucked in behind the sofa, the diminutive dining area is furnished with an oval pedestal table, two slim chairs, and a settee. A versatile piece that the family can use in a number of places in their next home, the settee can seat three adults comfortably and is less visually crowded than three chairs would be.

◁ As rents rise in New York, parents sleeping on a Murphy bed in the living room is an increasingly common set up—and it's a smart one: kids can go to sleep earlier in the bedroom and parents can stay up in the main living space and fold their bed down right before they go to sleep. Crystal purchased her wall bed from BredaBeds.

▽ A gallery ledge is a great choice for a small space because it allows you to change up your art whenever you like.

◁◁ The bunk bed from Oeuf was an investment but, as Crystal points out, it's easier to make room in the budget for some nice furniture when you don't have a huge home to furnish. The bunk bed not only gives the kids each a place to sleep, it also creates a play space below and a spot above for Owen to retreat to, away from his little sister, Elle.

◁ The only drawback to the family's set up is that the parents have to creep through their kids' room to use the bathroom at night—thankfully, both kids are good sleepers.

▽   Crystal stashes additional toys in two large lidded baskets—out of sight but immediately on hand if either child wants to play with something. A pair of CB2 bookshelves lends visual symmetry to the room while providing tons of storage for books and toys.

▷   As if giving Owen and Elle the bedroom wasn't unconventional enough, Crystal put a sofa in the kids' room too. It's a smart move for a family in a small space in which grown-ups spend a ton of time lounging in the kids' room. The sofa is a sleeper, so it also offers friends and family a place to stay when they visit.

Danielle and Kevin O'Shea are documenting their journey fixing up their mobile home, jobsite office trailer, and "weekend house" van on Instagram at @taking.it.tiny.

the unconventional solution

Santa Maria, California | Square Feet: 396

Danielle and Kevin O'Shea met in college in San Luis Obispo, and the couple bounced around Southern California after graduation. After several rentals, they were starting to itch for a place they could call their own, but real estate prices in Southern California made a home purchase out of reach. Around the same time, Danielle's mother had started a new business. Eager to lure her daughter back to her hometown to come work for her, Danielle's mom and dad proposed an unusual solution to their daughter and her fiancé: They'd provide a spot on their property for a very small home. The couple just needed to figure out a housing solution that would fall under four hundred square feet (the maximum size for an additional structure that wouldn't require special permits).

The couple explored many options, including a custom-built tiny house, a prefab home, a converted shipping container, and an RV. The solution came in the form of a 1994 Cavco Saguaro mobile home purchased off Craigslist. The mobile home had been sold along with a piece of land, and the new property owner was so eager to get rid of it that he sold it to Danielle and Kevin at a great price. Once in place on Danielle's parents' property, they connected the Saguaro to the septic system, well, and electricity—major projects that were mostly handled by hired professionals.

Within two years, Kevin and Danielle had landscaped the property and added a jobsite trailer as a separate office for Kevin, who works remotely for his company. They'd also almost paid off the costs to buy the mobile home and get it situated, allowing them to save for their forever home.

▷ The front door opens into a sliver of a hallway that connects all the areas of the home. A slender wall-mounted coat rack and a basket for shoes keep just a few essentials on hand.

▷▷ The corner kitchen has a full-size stove and a double sink beneath a window. A pullout cutting board to the left of the range can be used as an extra prep surface. The built-in spice rack keeps herbs and seasonings right at hand instead of lost in a jumbled cabinet.

▽   The dining table is compact but can seat six, and it doubles as Danielle's desk on days when she works from home.

▷   The main living area feels light and airy thanks to a fourteen-foot lofted ceiling, wrap-around windows, and a glass sliding door. The sideboard to the left of the sofa holds all manner of household essentials, including Tupperware, kitchen linens, tools, cookbooks, and one drawer dedicated to supplies for their dog, Rue.

The bedroom came with a mirrored closet big enough for two and a wall of built-in storage. Danielle and Kevin sacrificed the ability to walk around both sides of the bed for the comfort of a king-size mattress, which was key for Kevin, who is tall.

△ A single accent wall of wallpaper adds interest to the bedroom without overwhelming it—because of the mirrors, it actually feels like two walls of pattern.

▷▷ The Saguaro's bathroom design uses a clever trick: the sink vanity's counter extends over the top of the toilet to eke out extra surface area in the tiny bath. Danielle and Kevin installed two shelves above and put toiletries into chic vessels—giving the room more storage and style.

▷ A wall-mounted rack holds Danielle's necklaces, which double as decoration.

◁◁ Centered around a firepit, the outdoor seating area has a great view and connects the living and office spaces together.

▽ Kevin's office is actually a jobsite trailer (also purchased off Craigslist) normally used on construction sites.

They say a picture is worth a thousand words. So, a breathtaking vista may be worth a couple hundred square feet, especially when the view is through floor-to-ceiling windows like the ones in this apartment in Long Island City.

the rooms with a view

Queens, New York | Square Feet: 700

When Andres Ortega and Steven Butschi first met, Steven was living with family in Midtown and Andres in a tiny studio in Long Island City. Soon after Steven moved into Andres's place. As the couple soon discovered, a home never feels smaller than when two adults move in together for the first time (often you have doubles of practically everything!). So, they quickly upgraded to a cozy one bedroom, also in Long Island City.

The new apartment's bedroom was separated from the main living space by a hallway, which appealed to them because it made the sleeping area feel separate and private from the living space. Although small in size, their apartment feels downright luxurious thanks to floor-to-ceiling windows and just the right amount of space for everything.

A long-time employee of the retail company West Elm, Andres has an employee discount on the company's furnishings and an insider's knowledge of how the pieces work in real life. Andres carefully shopped his employer's offerings over time, always opting for things that he felt he could use in another space, since he and Steven knew the rental was not their long-term home. He was also strategic with his picks: a not-too-big seventy-eight-inch sofa, three occasional tables instead of a large coffee table, and a pedestal dining table that adds major style within a minimal footprint.

Shortly after we photographed their apartment for the book, Andres and Steven moved into a new apartment. Having mastered their previous small space, the couple went even smaller, but not as tiny as the first studio—it was the Goldilocks of apartments: just right. And Andres's furniture buying strategy paid off: he only had one piece of furniture that didn't work in the new space.

▷ With no proper vestibule or coat closet, Andres set up a landing spot for daily gear with a narrow console table with baskets below. When the men come home, they can quickly stash their bags, shoes, bike helmets, and more.

▷▷ Three wooden coat hooks, a pair of folding stools, and baskets give guests a place to comfortably transition into the home. Andres says he thinks of the area as a "prompt" for guests to hang their coats and sit down to take off their shoes.

◁ The expansive city skyline view makes the living room feel much larger than it really is. The Amigo Modern chair designed by Eric Trine is a style focal point, but because it has a wire frame it is visually light. To keep the space uncluttered, the couple is vigilant about what comes into their home and about making sure everything has a designated place.

▽ The hexagonal tables can be moved in different configurations when the couple entertains or if they need to make room for a guest on an air mattress.

▽ Andres and Steven liked the apartment's semi-open kitchen layout because it made the space feel larger while still keeping the kitchen separate from the main living area.

▷ When researching different dining tables for the space, Andres realized a round pedestal table would best let foot traffic flow around it. A model that was just forty-four inches left enough room for a small sideboard, which houses entertaining essentials and acts as a gallery space for some of the couple's art collection.

While the bedside tables do not match, both are made of glass, which keeps the room feeling light. However, the see-through design means they can't hide anything either, so a basket tucked under each one stores the usual detritus that would go in bedside table drawers. Wall-mounted sconces keep the bedside tables clear, and the Kevin Russ photograph above the bed offers an additional "view" in the small bedroom.

The apartment lacks a linen closet, but the bathroom is generous in size, so Andres and Steven are able to store their hamper, extra towels, and toiletries right in the bathroom.

▽ The couple sacrificed one of their three closets to store their bicycles—a perennial storage problem for bike-riding New Yorkers.

▷ A hallway dividing the bedroom from the main living space helps delineate public and private areas. On the left are the bike closet and the laundry closet, and on the right is the bathroom.

A rare commodity in New York City, Ellen's working fireplace lends her studio a homey feeling.

all the elegance, ¼ the space

Manhattan, New York | Square Feet: 400

Ellen O'Neill raised her daughter on New York's Upper East Side in a "classic six" apartment (a common layout with six rooms: a dining room, a living room, a kitchen, two bedrooms, plus a smaller "maid's bedroom"), but after she had divorced and her daughter had moved out, it felt like too much for one person—what Ellen describes as "the unique problem of too much space." At the time Ellen worked for a hotel chain and thought to herself, "I just want one perfect room." She also wanted to move downtown to a more creative neighborhood.

One New Year's Day, Ellen was reading the classified listings of the *New York Times* when she saw a posting for a studio on Gramercy Park North, one of the most coveted blocks in New York City for its proximity to the last private garden square in Manhattan *and* a key to enter the park. Curious, she arranged to see it the following Monday. She found a light-filled aerie with a wrap-around balcony: her perfect room. "I never looked back," she says of her decision to downsize fifteen years ago.

When it came time to decorate her new home, Ellen used her years of experience in retail and hotel design to create her dream. Her strategy: everything needed to go with everything else, so she could move things around without worrying about what matches with what. She stuck to a strict palette of black and white (a rule that also applies to her wardrobe), plus natural fibers and textures. With a lifetime of collected art and objects, the result is much more personal than any hotel room: an artistic garret with a hint of Ellen's uptown past.

▽   The entry table is an antique daguerreotype developing stand—its slots and trays are handy for corralling papers and other everyday essentials.

▷   Ellen hired a carpenter to build shelving into all the walls of the apartment entryway to store her books, magazines, and other reference materials.

"Design is coming to grips with one's real lifestyle, one's real place in the world. Rooms should not be put together for show but to nourish one's well-being."

ALBERT HADLEY

◁ Originally a maid's quarters, the apartment did not have a full kitchen when Ellen purchased it—just a sink and a giant refrigerator. With the help of an under-the-counter fridge, a bar-size sink, an eighteen-inch dishwasher, and a compact stove, she was able to fit a full cooking space into the niche off the main room. An existing skylight overhead illuminates the space.

▽ Ellen's generously sized bathroom possesses a full-size claw-foot tub and a window—making it more luxurious than what you'll find in many much larger apartments.

▽   The club chairs and sofa are small in scale, perfectly sized to the studio. All are antiques found on trips to Europe: older pieces are often good choices for small spaces because things were often built smaller then than they are today.

▷   When Ellen first moved into the apartment, she slept on a daybed that she used as a sofa by day. But she jokes that that got old pretty quickly. Ellen upgraded to a wrought-iron canopied bed that acts almost as a room within the main room.

◁◁ The desk is an old farmhouse table painted in Ellen's preferred palette of black and white. Ellen had the large bottle converted to a lamp to give her work area something with large scale; because the lamp is glass, it doesn't overpower the space.

◁ The hallway between the main room and the bathroom is lined with closets where Ellen stores her clothes. Ellen's collection of black-and-white photos, drawings, and prints turns the utilitarian space into an art gallery.

67

Just five feet wide at its widest point, Ellen's balcony wraps all the way around her apartment. During the warm months, she keeps her doors open all the time.

A neutral and natural palette and white-washed walls help to tie together the many antique and vintage finds in Glenn's cozy cottage.

the converted
artist's cottage

East Hampton, New York | Square Feet: 600

Designer Glenn Ban and his son Charlie live on the East End of Long Island, in a town known as a summer destination. The streets bustle with vacationers from Memorial to Labor Day, but their town becomes more like a sleepy New England village the rest of the year (Charlie's class at the local high school has fewer than twenty kids!).

A couple years ago, Glenn and Charlie moved from one small home in a nearby town to their current cottage. The little house is an auxiliary building to a larger one on the property, and it had traditionally been rented out to artists during the summer.

The cottage has a simple layout that grew from an original single-room structure, and Glenn did little more than add a coat of paint before moving into the house. It was a refreshingly small renovation for someone who earns a living making spaces beautiful, but Glenn is a master of elegantly elevating the humble. His home is a calling card for the curated look he is known for as a designer.

Filled with art and clean-lined furniture pieces from a variety of eras, the space is a lesson in both simplicity and sophistication. The bedrooms border on monastic in their pared-down aesthetic, and the living space has just the right amount of accessories and art to give it personality without feeling the least bit cluttered. Instead of worrying about the kitchen's humdrum cabinets, Glenn embraced the palette of white and natural wood and put the focus on a large-scale bookshelf filled with his enviable collection of kitchenware.

In an area that is known for its wealth and its mansions, Glenn's little cottage and his less-is-more décor are something of an anomaly, but Glenn says it's all he and his son really need.

A palette of black, white, and brown holds the many eras and styles of furnishings in Glenn's living room together. The stripes of the rug underfoot echo the repetition of the beams overhead.

▽   With limited shelf space, Glenn stores his design,
architecture, and art books in tidy stacks around the house.

▷   An iconic Saarinen table and a coat of white paint on the
floor instantly make this corner of the old house feel modern. The
corner hutch is an old-fashioned idea due for a modern revival
for its efficient used of an often-unused space.

◁   With not much storage space in the kitchen, Glenn decided to bring in an oversize bookcase to house his collection of kitchenwares and ceramics.

▽   Glenn just let his vintage kitchen be with no fuss about not having the latest look. His relaxed attitude is one that every small-space dweller should try to remember when assessing what needs to be done versus what would be nice to do someday.

◁ The Donald Judd-esque plywood daybed was built for Glenn's old home but fit almost perfectly in this corner of the enclosed porch.

▷ The opposite side of the porch has a built-in table and room to stash shoes beneath. Glenn displays a rotating collection of framed art and found objects above.

◁◁ Measuring just 7 ½' x 13' each, the two bedrooms are nearly identical in size and have little more than a bed and a closet in each.

◁ Glenn's son's room manages to look very "adult" because most of his youthful things, like video games and books, are at his other dad's house where he spends the weekends.

Jacqueline opted for a round table because it fit nicely in the center of the room (and it had no corners for kids to bonk their heads on). She did not install a pendant overhead so she could move the table during parties. But not every choice was purely space saving: Jacqueline loved the look of Hans Wegner's classic Wishbone chairs and chose them over slimmer chairs.

the "luxury of less" co-op

Brooklyn, New York | Square Feet: 675

You wouldn't know it by looking at her home today, but Jacqueline Schmidt was not a born minimalist: she once lived in a tchotchke-packed 1,200-square-foot loft. Reading a Terence Conran book one day, Jacqueline came across a passage that asked what would be left if you were to take everything out of your home, put it on your lawn, and only bring in what you needed. Thinking about necessity got her to assess *why* she needed so much space and so much stuff. Gradually, she sold off almost all of her books, art, art supplies, niche-use kitchen tools and appliances, and even furniture. She quickly fell in love with the freedom of owning less. "Getting rid of stuff is the easiest, most affordable way to create space," she says.

Jacqueline met and married a man who shared her desire to live small, and the two began to hunt for an apartment for their soon-to-be family of three. But this was in the notoriously competitive Brooklyn real estate market and they found themselves outbid on every place they liked. So they focused their hunt on the kinds of unrenovated apartments that brokers list with phrases like "Needs TLC" or "Bring your contractor!" The apartment they found was located right across from Prospect Park in Park Slope, but it was a mess and it was tiny—even by New York standards.

With a home finally secured, Jacqueline planned a new way of living. Jacqueline asked herself, "What if I only had what I needed? What if I based my choices on need, not want?" With this mindset, she carefully turned 675 square feet into a bright and airy two-bedroom home. Her plan relied on wall beds, built-in storage galore, and a commitment to living with less.

Five years later, life has brought many changes: a second child, a divorce, and a new career as the director of design for a co-living real estate developer, but the apartment has adapted handily to her family's changing needs.

Jacqueline reconfigured the kitchen as an efficient galley. The Fagor appliances are all designed for small spaces. The cabinets are IKEA, but she splurged on honed marble counters and backsplash to elevate the look and feel of the space.

◁   A cozy L-shaped sofa makes efficient use of the living room space while still comfortably seating all three family members plus guests. The wall-mounted sconce provides reading light without taking up any floor space.

▽   Even the window treatments have space-saving in mind: the simple roller shades take up no space and, when pulled all the way open, offer the largest possible view of Prospect Park across the street.

▽   Jacqueline commissioned a custom bookcase to fit the stretch of wall adjacent to her kitchen. The drawers conceal the everyday bits of life while the shelves allow Jaqueline to display some of the few things she kept after her big midlife decluttering.

▽   The sliding door that separates the bedroom from the living space is mounted on custom tracks from Cavity Sliders. The track embedded in the ceiling feels lighter and less cumbersome than a barn door, and when the door is open there is no division between the bedroom and the living space. While marble counters and fancy tiles fall into the nice-to-have category, mechanical elements like this sliding door hardware are a must-have. Likewise, Jacqueline made the decision to invest in expensive Resource Furniture beds instead of other lower-quality wall beds because she knew she'd be using them every day and needed them to last.

▷   A wall bed from Resource Furniture folds away to make the second bedroom all but disappear during the day. Built-in storage on either side of the bed houses Jacqueline's wardrobe.

◁ Jacqueline made room for play in her sons' 10' x 11' bedroom with foldaway bunk beds from Resource Furniture. Jacqueline had the beds installed with a soffit above for an almost seamless, built-in look.

▽ The small oak desk on the opposite side of the room is from Hübsch, a Danish company, and the wall-mounted storage is from Resource Furniture.

▷ The secret to Jacqueline's minimalist look is the full wall of storage that lines the entry hallway. Designed with slab doors and no handles, you are almost unaware of it as you pass through the space. Jacqueline measured to make room for suitcases, shoes, linens, and even cubbies for the vacuum and printer.

▷▷ Jacqueline gutted the bathroom and rebuilt it according to her philosophy of the "luxury of less." A marble tub surround, Ann Sacks wall tiles, and Kohler fixtures are all high-end choices that make the small room feel luxurious.

The exterior of the tiny house is wrapped in weathered cold-rolled steel siding. Leslie was drawn to the material for its complete lack of maintenance. Among Leslie's neighbors is this Tumbleweed Tiny House, whose owners use it as a weekend escape and an income-producing rental property.

the not-so-tiny tiny house

———

Fairplay, Colorado | Square Feet: 312

Leslie Rhyner had lived most of her life in the Chicago area, but after falling in love with the mountains, she knew she wanted to make her way out west. After retiring from teaching, Leslie moved to Colorado. Once there, Leslie happily settled into a two thousand-square-foot house and began working part-time in real estate. However, one night, Leslie tuned in to a tiny house television program and discovered an alternate world to the conventional homes she was selling and living in. Her curiosity piqued, Leslie dove head first into watching and reading anything she could find on the tiny house movement. Quickly, her home began to feel way too big.

Leslie started to dream about building her own tiny home—something she could easily maintain. However, when she began to research making her idea into a reality, she found that many tiny-home builders wouldn't customize their models to a homeowner's desires. She also discovered that it was hard to find places where it is legal to live in a tiny house full time.

Leslie's research led her to Greg Parham of Rocky Mountain Tiny Houses. Based in Durango, Colorado, Greg was close by and happy to help Leslie build her dream house. Their collaborative design is an eight-foot-wide tiny house built on a gooseneck chassis. Greg says many single people opt for just a twenty-four-foot-long house, but Leslie went for a thirty-one-foot design so she would have room to host guests comfortably, including her adult daughter. The master bedroom sits above the gooseneck and a second sleeping area is lofted over the kitchen space.

Leslie found the other key to her dream in the Whispering Aspen Village near Fairplay, Colorado. It's a mobile home community with a few dozen Park Model cabins, several RVs, and six tiny houses. As a landowner and board member of the homeowners association, Leslie is part of a small-living community that is hopefully paving the way for other legal tiny house communities.

Living tiny has allowed Leslie the financial freedom to travel more, including international trips with her daughter who lives in Europe. Located just a half hour from Breckenridge, Leslie is able to rent out her tiny house to visiting skiers whenever she's away.

The master sleeping loft is tall enough for Leslie to stand comfortably and is accessed by steps, not a ladder—two qualities that were musts for Leslie, who is in her sixties and hopes to age in place in her tiny home.

"It is the sweet, simple things of life which are the real ones after all."
LAURA INGALLS WILDER

▷ The "sladder" (steps-ladder) to the guest loft is a clever yet simple solution. A basic dowel design lets the ladder pivot from its folded-up position to its angled climbing position.

▷▷ Leslie fell in love with the Rocky Mountains and their breathtaking vistas.

▽ The secondary loft has a height of only three feet, but windows on three sides keep it from feeling claustrophobic.

The L-shaped kitchen is centered around a corner sink—with wraparound windows to give Leslie a view while doing dishes. With the fridge and stove to the left and counter space and pantry to the right, the kitchen forms a natural work triangle.

◁◁　A custom fold-down table gives Leslie a place to eat or work but can easily be folded away when she needs more floor space. IKEA makes a similar off-the-shelf version.

◁　In Leslie's bathroom design, the walls go all the way to the ceiling, which allows for a window at the top. Many tiny houses have some storage above the bathroom, but Leslie preferred a smaller bedroom over a cramped bathroom.

The architects' redesign put the house's entrance on the side, giving the family greater privacy from their tenants in front. The red painted door pops against the black siding.

the tenant-subsidized new-build

—

Santa Monica, California | Square Feet: 1,030

Polly Hall and Andrew Barkan didn't set out to build a new house, but that is practically what they ended up doing with their Los Angeles home when it came time to remodel. The couple had been living in a rental apartment on a property with two buildings (one two-family unit and a small house behind). While calculating how their family could afford to buy a home of their own, the rental setup made Polly realize that a home with multiple units could generate enough rental income to make it possible to more comfortably cover the large mortgage payment a house in Los Angeles demands. Figuring she had nothing to lose, Polly asked her landlord if he would consider selling her his property. To her surprise, he said yes.

After purchasing the property from their landlord, Polly and Andrew moved into the back house. With the birth of their son, Izzy, the couple began to realize that they'd like a little more space—especially if a hoped-for second child were to come along. What started out as a plan to enlarge the existing house became a much larger project when their architects, Claudia Wiehan and Cynthia Kraus of Open Haus Design, discovered they'd need to rebuild the foundation beneath the house. With the help of Open Haus, the couple devised a plan to turn their vintage bungalow into a modern 1,030-square-foot two-bedroom home—all while keeping enough of the existing structure to comply with local code.

Because they started essentially from scratch, with the house stripped down to the framing, the architects were able to build in closets and storage everywhere they could. They also made the house feel much larger by lofting the ceiling in the main living space and opening up the entire back of the house with glass doors. The house was not completed before Polly and Andrew's daughter, Gertie, was born, but the results were worth the wait. Their cottage is quintessential California indoor-outdoor living, where their small space seems infinitely larger because of its proximity to nature.

▽   The Dutch door allows light and air into the front hallway but keeps the children inside. The backside of the living room's storage unit has additional shelves that face into the entryway.

▷   A wall of custom storage divides the entryway from the living room. The open storage holds books, family mementos, and the TV. The L-shaped sofa helps to define the "living room" within the great room.

◁   To maximize their living space, Polly and Andrew chose to make their bedroom just big enough to house their king-size bed and storage for their clothes. Because the architects needed to keep much of the original exterior, the windows next to Polly and Andrew's bed were fitted into the opening for the original front door.

▽   The family's only full-size bath is accessible from both the parents' and kids' bedrooms. Known as a "Jack and Jill bathroom," the advantage to this setup is that it is an efficient use of the floor space. (You may remember the kids on the *Brady Bunch* lived with a similar arrangement—and Mr. Brady was an architect!).

◁   The family commissioned the top bunk built-in from their cabinetmaker. The storage bed below is made from IKEA components.

▽   The closet doors are covered with blackboard paint below and corkboard above to give the kids a gallery space on usually unused door surface. A tall and narrow dresser fits perfectly on the remaining wall space.

▽   Polly wanted an interior Dutch door on the kids' room so she could use the lower half like a baby gate to keep the kids inside, but still in sight.

▷ The couple has a band and a podcast for kids, and run a nonprofit for other youth-focused podcasters, so it's no surprise that they've made room for hundreds of records and children's books. The clever storage cubes from Simple Wood Goods can be arranged in many ways.

▽ With the help of a pocket door, Open Haus squeezed in a tiny half bath off the entryway. While the whole family shares a shower, a second toilet has proved super-helpful with two young kids in the home.

◁ Every small space should make space for its inhabitants' passions: in the case of this family, a piano was a non-negotiable.

▷ A wall coated with chalkboard paint acts as a message board and kids' art space in the entryway.

◁ Completely open to the rest of the living space, storage was essential in the kitchen. Open Haus and Polly worked together to create a place for everything, including a special cabinet just for the vacuum cleaner and cabinetry for the washer and dryer.

▷ The midcentury modern dining table moved with Polly and Andrew from their early days as a couple in Brooklyn. With no leaves installed it measures less than four feet, but it can extend to fit a dinner party's worth of guests.

◁ The hinged doors from Panoramic Doors, a Los Angeles–based manufacturer, allow the family to open the back of the house completely to the outdoors. Designed to slide along a track and pivot on a single hinge, Panoramic doors don't eat up the outdoor floor space in front of them, the way traditional bifolds do.

▽ The large window above the kitchen counter opens up and the countertop extends outdoors to create an indoor-outdoor bar.

"The architect should strive continually to simplify; the ensemble of the rooms should then be carefully considered that comfort and utility may go hand in hand with beauty."

FRANK LLOYD WRIGHT

The tiny vestibule has a coat closet to the left and a few hooks to the right. Shavonda extended the entry space into the living room with a shoe cabinet from IKEA (which she dressed up with stylish agate knobs) and a large round mirror above.

the downsizing dream bungalow

Sacramento, California | Square Feet: 1,200

Shavonda Gardner and her wife, Naomi, were living in a "normal" basic builder house when they decided to trade their cookie-cutter home for a smaller place with old-school charm. The couple and their two children downsized from 2,400 square feet to a 1,200-square-foot bungalow. The money they saved also allowed Shavonda to leave her full-time job to focus on raising their kids and her passion for design.

The small space didn't stop Shavonda from making bold choices with their décor—nor did it turn them into a family of minimalists. As Shavonda decorated the new house, she documented her DIY projects and design finds on her blog. Soon, many people were following along with what Shavonda dubbed #ourdownsizingjourney.

To make the two-bedroom home work for their family of four, Shavonda and Naomi took what had been the den and made it into their bedroom, and they gave their kids, Michael and Bryanna, the two "real" bedrooms.

Ever curious about design, Shavonda's vision for the cottage is constantly in flux: rugs move from room to room, furniture shuffles places, and everything is always being tweaked and updated. This nimble attitude toward décor is part of what makes the small space work for her and her family.

Living small has meant that there's no place to hide while one space is under construction. For example, when Shavonda renovated their only bathroom, the family had to rely on the kindness of neighbors, who let them use their bathroom, and use the laundry room basin for sink showers. But the family feels the benefits of their smaller home far outweigh the drawbacks. Among the many pluses of their smaller space, Shavonda has gained such a large following that she is now a professional design blogger.

▽   The dining alcove has built-in storage. However, while the round table offers seating for up to six people, the one thing Shavonda does miss from their old house is the huge dinner table they used for entertaining.

▷   The family's living room is a lesson in why you shouldn't be afraid to go bold with your décor in a small space: the black walls create a moody vibe that anchors the rest of the house.

◁ Naomi and Shavonda get to sleep with a view of their large backyard in what was formerly a den. While the room is generously sized, the alcove where the bed sits offers just enough space for the bed and two night tables. Shavonda tucked two baskets beneath a bench at the foot of the bed to hold shoes.

▷ Tucked into a corner, Naomi's colorful sneaker collection is on full display in this shoe rack from IKEA. It's an example that almost anything displayed neatly can feel like a part of the décor.

▽ The couple got lucky when they discovered that IKEA's Pax wardrobes fit nearly perfectly along the long wall in their bedroom, which has no existing closets. The four side-by-side units offer more storage than even a fancy walk-in closet.

▷   Hallways are often ignored, which is exactly why Shavonda felt this was a great place to go bold with her wallpaper choice. She says, "How fun is it to have something interesting to experience when passing through from room to room?"

▷▷   A recent renovation brought the 1940s bathroom into the present with new tile, wallpaper, a sink vanity, and more, but the biggest change was the addition of an operable skylight. Bringing light and air into the bathroom made more of a difference than any extra storage or additional space could have brought.

◁◁ Shavonda used a host of small-space tricks to make her petite cook space work, including a hard-working island from a restaurant supply store, a hanging pot rack, and tons of wall-mounted storage. But perhaps most surprising of all, she opted for an eighteen-inch dishwasher instead of a full-size model. She finds that this size is just right for a day's worth of dishes and is happy to have the extra cabinet space.

◁ When Shavonda was renovating the kitchen, she was determined to keep the built-in spice rack and ironing board that were original to the house. (Hooray for 1940s small-space hacks!) "I basically planned the whole kitchen around that spice rack," she laughs.

▽ One of Shavonda's favorite ways to add color to a room is to paint the ceiling. Both the kids' rooms have white walls and colored ceilings.

▷ Shavonda's biggest tip for making a small room work for kids is to limit their stuff. In Michael's room, Shavonda used carpet tiles from Flor to create a rug that fit the small space perfectly.

◁◁ Want a guaranteed way to make laundry a less dreaded chore? Wallpaper your washroom in the brightest, boldest wallpaper you can find, like Shavonda did here. To make this room work harder, she also installed a long, narrow shelf above the machines and uses the area as her potting shed.

◁ In warm months, Shavonda and her family treat the covered patio as an extra room.

"The true secret of happiness lies in taking a genuine interest in all the details of daily life."
WILLIAM MORRIS

It was a new mothers group meeting in this neat-as-a-pin living room that launched Shira's career as a professional organizer: the other moms wanted Shira to help make their homes feel as calm and relaxing as hers.

the pro organizer's home base

Berkeley, California | Square Feet: 1,200

As a professional organizer, Shira Gill spends her days helping clients declutter their homes and set up systems to make their lives run more smoothly—often preventing the need to upgrade to a larger space. Shira has applied her skills to her own home to create a space that feels light, airy, and generous in size. In fact, a visitor to the Gill family's home might be surprised to hear it called small: from the outside, it looks like an average-size house, but the thirty-foot façade does not reveal that the house is only twenty feet deep.

At twelve hundred square feet, the house is not tiny, but unlike many family homes, the vintage Craftsman has just one full bathroom, one non-bedroom closet, and no attic or garage (aka no place to hide any clutter). Plus, with two school-age daughters and a business run from home, every part of the house is in active use, making its zen-like vibe all the more surprising.

The family's home is also a lesson in knowing when it's time to adapt and adjust what's not working—a key skill for any small-space dweller. Shira is constantly changing the space in both minor ways (a new office arrangement) and major ways (knocking a wall out between the kitchen and dining room).

Because their home is so orderly and free from clutter, the family is able to rent it out when they travel, offsetting the costs of their vacations: a true example of how living small can mean living large.

▽ The positioning of an L-shaped sofa and the sideboard behind it cleverly creates an "entryway" in the space.

▷ In the dining area, the house's original built-in storage houses all Shira's entertaining items: dishes, table linens, and more. A bench can be pulled up to one side of the table to allow the family to squeeze in an extra guest (or two extra kids) for meals.

◁   When Shira confided in an interior designer friend that she felt she'd have to move if she ever wanted to get her dream kitchen, the designer quickly suggested removing a wall between the kitchen and dining room and giving the newly adjoined spaces a coat of white paint for the fresh, light look Shira desired.

▽   The kitchen retains some of its original cabinetry, but has been further refreshed with quartz counters, updated lighting, and new appliances. Sometimes an outside eye is needed to see the potential in a small space—even when, like Shira, your job is making the most of existing spaces.

▷ True story: When looking through photos of Shira's home, I wasn't sure if she was married because I saw no obvious evidence of a spouse in the images. She told me that yes, her husband, Jordan, existed, but when I pressed further to say, "Well, what does *his* closet look like?" Shira texted me a photo of the other side of her maniacally ordered and minimalist closet—and it was almost as neat as Shira's. (You can see it on page 200.)

▷▷ Shira and Jordan took the smaller bedroom to let the girls have more room to spread out. Shira points out that the only thing they really do in the bedroom is sleep, so a smaller space is not really an issue.

◁   Shira uses the small third bedroom as her office. The matching Parsons desks look like a single unit when pushed together, while the linen-covered pinboard almost disappears into the wall painted a similar hue.

▽   While Shira has been tempted to decorate her daughters' shared room to cater to their latest interests, she's stuck to the neutral, timeless palette of the rest of the house—with little dashes of the hot pink they love.

▽ Tucked behind the living room at the back of the kitchen, this hardworking corner houses a teeny-tiny bathroom (a toilet in a closet and a sink just outside) that comes in handy when the Gills entertain. Shira installed a panel of stainless steel to act as a magnetic bulletin board.

▽ Shira lives by the classic organizing mantra: a place for everything and everything in its place, and when you see how organized the family's only shared closet looks, you understand why. Constant editing and conscious styling make even utilitarian spaces photo worthy.

▷ The recently renovated bathroom is outfitted with simple but smart storage solutions, including a hook rail, built-in niches for shampoo in the shower stall, and a minimalist bathroom vanity with storage.

Just because you live in a tiny space doesn't mean you have to have small-scale art. I spent years scouring eBay for this huge, vintage Rand McNally star chart, and today it is the focal point of my living room.

living small
headquarters

Queens, New York | Square Feet: 690

Welcome. This is my own little house in the city. I included my own home in this book to show you that I am living the small life too—along with my son and photographer husband, Weston Wells, who took the photographs for this book.

When we toured our Jackson Heights apartment with a real estate broker, it was being marketed as a one bedroom, but my husband took one look at the dining alcove and saw a second bedroom for our soon-to-arrive child. We also saw the building's shared garden as additional living space that wasn't officially part of our floor plan.

Because we'd saved on the purchase price, we had some money to update the kitchen and bathroom, refinish the floors, and install new barn doors on that dining alcove (hello, second bedroom!).

By choosing this small space, we chose to live with less. We committed to living within our means. We've been here almost five years, and in that time, we've tinkered with our small space plenty—adding the dishwasher we realized we needed once we had a kid of our own and installing extra shelving in an unassuming corner. It's a little laboratory of living small. I hope you'll enjoy what you find. Come on in.

◁ Our living space works extra hard. It is our living room, dining room, playdate central, and my husband's home office. The sofa is the only piece of furniture that we bought new and we made sure that it was actually comfortable enough for a guest to sleep on, since we don't have a guest bedroom.

▽ Purchased to fit a narrow space in an old apartment, this antique desk always manages to fit into our homes because of its slim profile; it offers a ton of storage and a place for me to work from home.

△   Weston's "office" is tucked into a corner of our living room. The corner desk unit is a hand-me-down from my parents' home that fits nearly perfectly into the space. Because it hugs the wall, the desk takes up very little floor space while offering the storage and surface area of a much larger desk.

▷   Most nights, our dinner guests are just my husband, my son, and my father-in-law who lives nearby, but when we have extra guests, we pull the pedestal table away from the window to seat up to seven people.

◁◁   We started from scratch with our kitchen because the previous layout was so inefficient. The redesigned kitchen has standard twenty-four-inch-deep cabinets on the stove side but only fifteen-inch-deep cabinets on the opposite side. We made one after-renovation addition: we installed the under-sink dishwasher (the Spacemaker by GE) after seeing one in a house we rented.

◁   A narrow mirrored backsplash opens up the feel of the room.

▷ Formerly a dining alcove, we installed sliding barn doors to close off the room as our bedroom. At just 8' x 10' feet, our room is very small. However, with six built-in drawers, the bed holds all of our folded clothing.

▽ We had the floating nightstands custom made by Etsy vendor Tim O'Brien Woodworks after we couldn't find off-the-shelf ones that would fit the space. In lieu of a proper hamper, we each have a small basket beneath our nightstands. The wall sconces leave the tabletops clear.

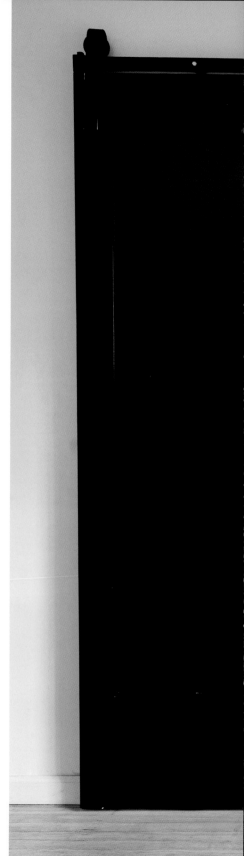

◁　When we moved in, we put our son in the former dining alcove bedroom, but when he was nearing a year old, we swapped the rooms when we realized we were often waking him up with our noise in the living room. Swapping rooms also got the kid gear out of our main living space.

▽　The six-drawer dresser is a more grown-up piece that will grow with our son, but it also did a fine job of holding diapers when he was a baby.

At first glance, our bathroom doesn't seem particularly small, but that's by design. We had to seek out the tiniest sink we could find and opted for a toilet with a petite profile.

"Small rooms or dwellings discipline the mind, large ones weaken it."

LEONARDO DA VINCI

Our building dates back to the 1940s when apartments were still graced with formal entryways. A sideboard holds all our entertaining essentials: China, wineglasses, linens—and our modem and router. The large mirror—a twenty-dollar Craigslist find—makes the room feel larger than it really is.

solutions

Whether you live in a one-room studio or a three-bedroom house, the actions of daily life are the same. Use these tips to pare back your belongings, make smart furniture choices, and refresh your space. The big and little solutions will help you sleep, eat, work, and play with ease in whatever space you have.

downsize & declutter

The fastest, easiest way to make your space feel more spacious is to declutter. Period. Less stuff equals more space. Whether it's a once-in-a-lifetime Kondo-style purge or a weekend here and there of editing, decluttering is key to living small.

THE SMALL SOLUTIONS

Downsizing will not happen overnight, but you can get started down the path to less with creative ways to jump-start the decluttering process.

Timer/Pomodoro Technique Set a timer for a period of time in which you go through a room looking for items to throw away, recycle, or donate, as well as items to be returned to their proper places. Don't do anything else (check you phone, get a snack, etc.) while the timer is running. Set it for twenty-five minutes, take a five-minute break, and start again.

One Item a Day Commit to getting rid of one item every day for a month (or longer!).

Gone Boxing Place a box in every room that needs decluttering and every time you find something that you're ready to part with, place it in the box. At the end of the month, go through and weed out anything that should be put in the trash and take the rest to your local charity.

20-20-20 Challenge Locate twenty items to throw away, twenty items to donate, and twenty items to be returned to their proper homes.

Photographic Evidence Take photos of your home to gain a fresh perspective on where clutter lurks. Decorator Celerie Kemble once told me that looking at photographs of my home would help me with the finishing touches to my décor, but when I tried it, I found it surprisingly effective for decluttering! Don't believe me? Snap photos of your space and you may be surprised at how untidy it really looks.

Snowball Method Get rid of one thing on Day One, two things on Day Two, three things on Day Three, and so on. Aim for twenty-one days of the snowball method for your first effort. If it feels easy, start over with Day One and try a full month next time.

Buddy System This is one of the most effective ways to declutter. Choose one of the methods above and agree

◁ Decluttering will reward you with a sense of calm and contentment. A bedroom like Shira Gill's that is free of clutter and the detritus of delayed decisions is a more peaceful place to lay your head each night. It's also infinitely easier to keep dust-free, another boon to healthy sleep.

on a plan with a friend, then text each other pictures of what you're throwing away or donating each day. My friends and I have done this with the snowball method and it is a magic bullet of motivation.

THE BIG SOLUTIONS

Change your relationship to the stuff. Decluttering and getting rid of excess is vital to living small, but more important still is to change how you think about possessions. To keep your closet from filling right back up after you've edited it down, you need to stop purchasing more clothes. To keep the kitchen from overflowing, you must resist the urge to buy another cute cutting board/tray/tea towel at a home goods store. Here are a few ways to help you adopt a less-is-more mindset.

Always shop with a list—and stick to it. It will help prevent you from overspending and acquiring things you don't need.

Distance yourself. Unsubscribe from all the retailer email lists you're on and call to be removed from catalog mailings too. Stop following brands on social media or, if you're really looking to disconnect, take a break from social media altogether.

> "For every minute spent in organizing, an hour is earned."
> BENJAMIN FRANKLIN

Employ the 24-hour rule. If you see something you really think you need, bookmark it or ask a store to put it on hold for you. Then wait a day to see how you feel. Chances are the "need" might be less pressing than you think.

Use what you've got. Sometimes the urge to buy something new is really just a desire for a change. You can find novelty in the things you already own. Take a colorful bedspread and drape it over your living room sofa. Open up your closet and spend a half hour writing down new outfit combinations. Take everything off your fridge door—or alternatively, cover it with a few beautiful photos. Move your furniture around—even if you end up moving it all back to its original spot, you've at least experienced a shift in perspective.

Stop shopping. If you cut out browsing stores for leisure, you're way less likely to bring home things you don't need. I was never the type to go to the mall or spend an afternoon at boutiques, but I used to go to the flea market every weekend. I still love secondhand markets and thrift stores, but now I limit my trips and try to enjoy the fun of finding things—not actually taking them all home.

Give differently. Help stop the culture of living large by gifting experiences instead of things. Or if you prefer to place an object in someone's hand, make it something consumable, like food, flowers, or special soaps.

Say no to freebies. This is where even avowed minimalists can get into trouble. When something is free, it is *so* hard to pass it up. But even a free object comes with a price tag: it's going to need dusting and cabinet space.

Edit every day. No matter how vigilant you are about keeping clutter out of your life, it has a sneaky way of returning. Magazines pile up, party favors creep in, socks go missing, pens migrate home from the office. If you do a sweep each night and put things back in their places, you'll be able to zero in on new clutter and keep the pileup at bay.

"The secret of happiness, you see, is not found in seeking more, but in developing the capacity to enjoy less."

SOCRATES

furnish

Buy furniture strategically and think carefully about the future uses of each piece you buy. Smart choices in furniture can go a long way toward making your tiny digs look larger, but don't feel like you have to buy everything specifically designed with small-space living in mind.

When shopping, ask yourself if you can imagine a piece of furniture in another home down the line. My mother bought a double bed with three built-in drawers for her apartment when she moved to New York City in the early 1970s, and it has moved at least a dozen times since and spent nearly a decade in my own city apartments. Talk about something that was built to last! Here are some universal tips to consider when choosing furniture for your space.

Stay simple. Stick to furniture that has clean lines and uncomplicated design. Opting for a simpler design will make your space feel light. Keep in mind that simple doesn't have to mean modern and sleek: the Shakers and Scandinavians have long been known for their simplistic design.

Beware of mirrored glass. A well-positioned mirror makes a room look larger, but a mirrored piece of furniture can make a room look cluttered when it reflects its surroundings.

Pick petite seating. In a small home, a love seat or settee is often a better choice than a full-size sofa. Not only will the smaller sofa fit better in your diminutive digs, but it will be a piece that you can use later if you graduate to more space. A love seat could live in a bedroom at the foot of a bed or as an accessory seating paired with a full-size sofa.

Go low. Look for furniture that sits closer to the ground. By choosing low-slung pieces, you'll open up space above giving a lofty feeling. Platform beds and slipper chairs are examples of pieces that are typically a few inches shorter than their counterparts. You can also use a saw to shorten the legs of a wooden table, bed, or chair to DIY your own low look—just be sure to measure precisely.

Think clearly. Make some of your furnishings practically disappear. Choose see-through furnishings, including glass, Lucite, and acrylic pieces, to open up a cramped space. As a bonus, clear furniture looks great with almost any style of décor.

◁ In this living room, the homeowners, Maria Salazar Ferro and John Uhl, chose a Lucite coffee table and a slightly smaller leather sofa—two furniture choices that leave the room feeling less crowded.

Clockwise from top left: An oval pedestal table takes up little floor space but makes room for a dinner party's worth of guests; a chair and dresser with slim legs have an airy feeling; a stack of iconic Stool E60s designed by Alvar Aalto; a custom-built desk makes this tiny corner into a workspace.

Go camping. Pieces designed for the outdoors and camping can be great choices for tight spaces: they're usually lightweight, small in scale, and often foldable.

Gather 'round. There are many dining table options for a small space, including special tables that fold away when not in use and those that expand with the addition of a leaf, both of which I've used in different apartments. However, perhaps the most versatile solution is a round pedestal table. Round tables are best because they take up less floor space than their rectangular counterparts while offering just as much seating. The choice of a pedestal design over one with multiple legs means that you can squeeze in extra diners when needed. The more streamlined look of a pedestal also provides less visual clutter. A forty-two-inch table can fit four, but if you have room for a forty-eight-inch one, you'll be able to comfortably seat six for a sit-down meal (and as many as eight if your friends don't mind getting cozy).

Stack 'em up. Furniture pieces that stack are a boon for a small space: Stools or dining chairs that can pile on top of one another, such as the classic Stool 60 designed by Alvar Aalto, take up the floor space of a single seat when not in use. Nesting side tables can expand or contract as needed.

White it out. A coat of white paint isn't just a fix for walls: it's also a great way to lighten up secondhand furniture. White reflects light and gives a sense of openness, making it a great choice for small spaces. If you've got white walls, white and ivory-hued furnishings will blend in with their surroundings and make the space look more expansive.

Show some leg. A sofa with visible legs takes up less visual space than one of an equal size with a skirt that comes to the floor. Likewise, a chest of drawers that is raised up on short legs seems airier than one that is solid all the way to the base. If you're buying a secondhand upholstered chair or sofa that you plan to make over, consider recovering it in a way that reveals the legs.

"I believe in plenty of optimism and white paint, comfortable chairs with lights beside them."

ELSIE DE WOLFE

renovate

Renovation is intimidating—but customizing your space is one of the most efficient ways to max out a home's potential. I know this from firsthand experience: I've made alterations to all of the homes I've lived in. In the pages that follow, I offer solutions for specific areas of your home (such as bedrooms, the kitchen, and home office), but to begin, here is advice that applies to all the parts of your home—whether it's a rental or your forever home.

THE SMALL SOLUTIONS

Let in the light. Take down whatever blinds or shades came with your place. Wash the windows (inside and out) and let the light shine in. If you feel exposed without the blinds, try self-adhesive privacy film: you can obscure the view into your home without losing any daylight. Basic options like a frosted glass look-alike are available at hardware stores and Stick Pretty sells sophisticated patterns.

Create faux built-ins. Use simple off-the-shelf bookcases as the foundation for "built-in" storage. If you're handy you can add your own trim, or you can hire a carpenter to finish it for you.

Upgrade your light fixtures. Replace your drab overheads. It's easy enough for a moderately handy person to do, and they can truly transform a space. If you rent, keep the old fixtures and swap them back out when you go. Or simply remove the covers on the existing lights and replace them with paper globes, which cast a soft, flattering light.

Assess the true cost of a costly update. Purchasing a Murphy bed or other pricey furniture piece for a rental may seem foolish but pause to consider the cost over time. If you could save four hundred dollars a month by renting a studio instead of a one bedroom, and a $1,200 Murphy bed will make the studio livable for two people, think of the investment as the equivalent of three months of the cheaper rent or mortgage payment.

Talk to your landlord. If there's a particular upgrade you're dying to make to your rental, speak with the owner. Perhaps if you pay for the labor, he or she will cover the costs of the materials. Or maybe you can skip one month's rent payment if you offer to regrout the whole bathroom. I know one architect who avoided years of rent increases on her affordable apartment by updating

◁ Shavonda Gardner has renovated her kitchen bit by bit over several years, making each improvement as she could afford it and DIYing whatever she could to keep costs down. Decorator tricks like the herringbone tile pattern and the Semihandmade cabinet doors give the space a high-end look.

the kitchen herself. Another friend got the bathroom of his dreams for just the cost of the plumber (he talked his landlord into paying for the new sink vanity and toilet).

THE BIG SOLUTIONS

Make your space feel bigger—without expanding the footprint. There are plenty of ways to give your home the illusion of extra space. These mini renovations make a big difference in what it feels like to be inside your space.

Hunt for rooms. Could your closet become a nursery? Or your dining alcove a small bedroom? Could a built-in desk make your entryway double as a home office?

Do some detective work. Find out what's behind your walls. Would removing the dropped ceiling give you a few more inches overhead? Could exposing the brick give just a little more breathing room? Are there non-load-bearing walls you could knock out?

Expand your openings. To open up the space without knocking down entire walls, consider heightening door-ways and installing larger windows.

Aim for the rafters. Vaulting a ceiling will make your space feel much larger. It's also an excellent opportunity to add skylights to maximize interior natural light.

Sneak in storage everywhere. A narrow bookcase at the end of a hall, cubbies in the entryway, shelving in a headboard—there's almost no place that's not ripe for additional storage.

---

sometimes don't ask, and just do.

I've broken the rules on plenty of leases by painting walls a color (forbidden!) and even painting some particularly ugly kitchen cabinets white, yet I've never been charged a fee upon moving out. In fact, my very first apartment was in such bad shape when we signed the lease that we refinished the floors, spackled, and painted the whole place (thank you to my old roommate's mom, Patricia, for the help!). It was a lot of work, but we knew the rent was incredibly cheap for the location, so it was worth the time and money. Decorator William McLure was even bolder with a former rental, in which he ripped out the carpets (sneaking it out piece by piece in the trash) and painted the subfloors white. You know your landlord best, so proceed with caution.

Build in flexibility. When designing built-in book-shelves, opt for ones with movable (rather than fixed) shelves so you can adjust your storage space as needs change.

Go vertical. Take bookcases and kitchen cabinets all the way to the ceiling to maximize your storage space. (You'll never miss that awkward space above your kitchen cabinets, I promise.)

Clockwise from top left: A vaulted ceiling makes a room feel large; storage built in on both sides of a kitchen island; cabinets installed with no gap overhead; a filing cabinet embedded in a banquette seat.

10 things to do before embarking on any remodel

Whether you're thinking of buying a home that needs TLC or are planning to update your current space—and whether you're a first-time renovator or a borderline flipper—there are some rules of thumb that you should follow.

1. Create a wish list. Write down every last thing that you would like to do. You can prioritize these desires later.

2. Get quotes and research costs for everything on your wish list; be as detailed as possible. Don't forget to account for paint, grout, and other basic supplies. Shipping costs must also be included (for example, shipping tile can cost almost as much as the tile itself). You may also be pleasantly surprised by some items, like I was when I found out refinishing our floors would be just a couple hundred dollars.

3. Make a budget—and plan to exceed it. I have yet to hear of a renovation that did not cost more than the homeowner planned.

4. Consider hiring an architect. Even for a job as small as a galley kitchen, an architect's expertise can make the most of your renovation budget and help you avoid mistakes.

5. Measure everything twice, if not three times, especially if you're not using an architect.

6. Do it all at once. What you plan to do later will almost certainly turn into what you do never.

7. Don't start until you're ready. Waiting until you have saved the money, made all the decisions, created a schedule, and ordered the supplies will ensure a smoother process.

8. Find a crash pad. Renovation is dirty and chaotic. It may seem like a cost-saver to try to live in your house during renovation (I know, I've tried it myself), but if there's any way to relocate temporarily, the work will go faster with your family off-site and you'll maintain your sanity.

9. Make a time line. Clear, established due dates will help keep contractors on track. Don't be afraid to speak up when deadlines are missed!

10. Introduce yourself. Even if your contractor is managing the subcontractors, it pays to know each and every person who will be working on your home. Get their contact information too, in case you want to hire them again at a later date.

Stop swinging. Traditional doors take up a whole lot of floor space. Replace interior doors with pocket or barn doors, consider a curtain on a closet opening, or go without a door altogether. In my own apartment, swapping a barn door for the existing French ones on my tiny bedroom was key to making my small space work.

SMALL-FOOTPRINT RENOVATIONS

I believe that living small is more than just choosing a tiny space: it's about living lightly on the Earth and being mindful of the resources you use. Think small when deciding what needs renovating or replacing in the first place. The reality show mentality of a full makeover is the same mindset that believes we need to live in larger houses and drive bigger cars. Maybe your bathroom doesn't need to be gutted down to the studs; perhaps a new vanity, some fresh grout, and new hardware are all your space needs to be enough. Maybe you don't need to enlarge the footprint of your kitchen if you rethink the layout. This is what living small is all about: deciding what is enough and what is excess.

When it is time to embark on your project, research and source earth-friendly materials. Keep these tenants in mind:

Use upcycled materials. Shop the salvage yard before the big-box home improvement store. Try to renew what you've already got before scrapping it in favor of something new.

Ditch the chemicals. Choose low- and zero-VOC paints, which are a little more expensive, but since you're using them in a smaller space, try to justify the splurge.

Be choosy about wood. Skip the chemical-laden pressure-treated wood and avoid particle board at all costs; instead look for FSC-certified and reclaimed woods or renewable bamboo.

Recycle your waste. You may be surprised which of your discards other people may want and what pieces of the trash can be recycled. For example, Carpet Cycle collects and recycles old wall-to-wall carpet on the East Coast. Habitat ReStore, a retail outlet that raises funds for Habitat for Humanity, accepts building materials, appliances, and kitchen cabinets as donations. Over the years, I have been truly amazed by what people will take from you if you post it on the "free" section on Craigslist.

Explore energy-efficient upgrades. Big-ticket renovations with an eye toward energy savings may feel daunting, but if you're planning to stay in your house for the long haul, they will likely pay off. Maybe you can afford new energy-efficient windows or additional insulation because you didn't spend your extra dollars on extra rooms. If you're really dedicated to clean energy, geo-thermal heating, solar panels, and even a wind turbine are next-level ways to update your home.

"Good houses take work."
MICHAEL S. SMITH, DECORATOR

sleep

*Of all the rooms in a small home, a tiny sleeping space shouldn't be a big challenge:
you need room for a bed and little more. Of course, many of us have bedrooms that
do double-duty as a place to work, a space to play, and a home to our wardrobes.
As you tackle your "sleep" space, focus on the part of the room that is devoted to rest
and then address the additional functions with tips from the following chapters.*

While your bedroom may need to serve more than one function, it should not be a repository for all the things that don't have a proper home (luggage, the laundry basket, boxes waiting to be returned). As you plan your small-space sleep area, minimize it to what it is truly meant to be: a place to rest and a refuge from the world. That doesn't mean it needs to be minimalist in style: if you like stacks and stacks of books and piles of pillows, go for it, just ask yourself if each item contributes to a feeling of restfulness.

Legendary decorator Billy Baldwin believed the bedroom should be the most personal room in the house, and I agree. This is the room to indulge your whims and display your favorite family photographs. Fill your room with things that bring you joy, so you'll wake up to things that make you smile each day.

THE BIG SOLUTIONS

The largest solution in any sleep space is the place you actually lay your head. While a bedroom needs little more than a bed, I do advocate for one that makes the best use of the space it takes up, like a Murphy bed or a storage bed. Consider this: In 2017, Manhattan's real estate clocked an average of $1,773 per square foot. Meaning the twenty-eight square feet of space for a full-size bed has net worth of nearly fifty thousand dollars in New York City. *Fifty thousand dollars!* Put that valuable real estate to work with one of these solutions:

Beds with Drawers A bed frame with built-in drawers is a great way to put your sleeping space to use. My husband and I have a wooden captain's bed with six drawers built into the frame, which allows us to store all our folded clothing right in our tiny bedroom—without the help of a chest of drawers. Storage beds are also great for guest rooms because you can store the room's extra linens in the drawers and leave your guests the bureau drawers to use. In a kid's room, a bed with drawers can store toys.

Wall beds Also known as Murphy beds, wall beds are a godsend for small spaces. In my early twenties, I invested in a Murphy bed for a 225-square-foot studio. With the

◁   In my own home, our bedroom just fits a queen-size bed and two wall-mounted bedside tables. At
8' x 10' it is very small, but it's enough. A painting by my grandfather holds a place of honor above the bed.

foldaway bed I had both a living space and a sleeping space in my single room. (I promise, Murphy beds are just as comfortable as regular beds.) They are also handy for families looking to stay in a beloved home after the arrival of children. My sister and her husband spent three years sleeping on one in their one-bedroom apartment's living room, giving their kids the bedroom.

Storage beds A mattress frame with a lift-up design and storage beneath is another clever option. Know that this style is more practical for storing things you only need to access occasionally, like out-of-season clothes, luggage, or seasonal décor—not your everyday wardrobe.

Loft beds A loft bed is a feature in many tiny houses. A loft is an efficient way to make use of vertical space. If you have generous ceiling height, as my first apartment did, you can get two "rooms" into the space of one. However, as a former loft-bed dweller, I can tell you there are drawbacks: you *will* bonk your head, climbing up and down the ladder in the middle of the night is tiresome, and making your bed is a challenge. But for some spaces, a loft makes the most sense.

Some practical consideration: A loft should have at least fifty-two inches of height below to sit at a desk and a minimum of sixty-eight inches to stand (eighty inches would be more comfortable though). Above, you'll need thirty inches from the top of the mattress to the ceiling to give you space to sit up comfortably. If you're building your own loft, don't feel constrained by the sizes that mattresses come in. My loft was an awkward size, but instead of sleeping on a smaller twin mattress, I had a foam mattress cut to somewhere in between a twin and a full, and just tucked a full fitted sheet in beneath it to make the bed.

Lofts can also be retrofitted into small houses where there is unused space beneath the eaves. Architect Jessica Helgerson did this in her Sauvie Island, Oregon, home, sneaking in a major "found" room in a home with a mere 540-square-foot footprint.

Cribs When choosing a crib for your child, consider how long you plan to stay in your home. A mini crib takes up considerably less space than a standard crib, but your child will only be able to use it for approximately their first year to year and a half of life. If you're considering a traditional-size crib, look for one with a storage drawer below. Under-crib drawers are a great place to store extra diapers and wipes, which take up more room than new parents often anticipate because they are so much cheaper to purchase in bulk.

Toddler Beds Purchasing a toddler bed can seem like a waste of money, since it will be used for such a relatively short period, but the pint-size bed buys you space and time! A child can sleep in a toddler bed for several years, and it saves so much floor space that it may mean your family can comfortably stay in a smaller home longer. Just know that most crib mattresses are very firm (to make them safe for babies to sleep on), so your bigger kid may need a mattress upgrade or a cushiony topper to make the former crib mattress comfortable.

"The details are not the details. They make the design."

CHARLES EAMES

Clockwise from top left: A queen-size Murphy bed, a storage bed from IKEA, a toddler-size bed, and a lofted bunk bed from Ouef.

a word about bedroom materials

Adults spend approximately one third of their day in their beds, and for young kids it's even more. This should serve as motivation to closely consider the products you use in your bedroom. I argue for using eco-friendly materials everywhere in the home, but they are especially important in the bedroom. Look for paints labeled low- and no-VOC, research mattresses that are made without flame retardants or polyurethane foam, choose hardwoods over composites, and opt for bedding made from natural fibers like organic cotton, linen, and wool.

Trundle and Bunk Beds If you have multiple children, or are likely to host guests, a trundle or bunk (or combination of the two) is a wise choice. If you'll be using both beds every day, a bunk is a more practical choice than a trundle, but if you will only use the second bed occasionally, then a trundle will keep the overhead space in your room open. To get three beds into the square footage that one occupies, a bunk bed with a built-in trundle will do the trick.

Bunk beds also come in alternative sizes, like twin-over-full models or L-shaped triple and quadruple bunks. If you have a house with only one guest room, one of these three-person-plus bunks can help you host visiting families in a single room. They are often an investment at a thousand dollars or more but, remind yourself, they are a tiny fraction of the cost of a whole additional guest room.

THE LITTLE SOLUTIONS

Bedding

While it might not seem like your bedding has anything to do with space optimization, the look of your bed can have a big impact on your home. In a small studio apartment, the bed may be the largest surface in the room. Plain white linens feel airy, but a bold pattern gives your room a focal point and makes it feel more designed. Personally, I lean more toward the light and white, but small spaces can accommodate all styles.

Whatever you choose, try to limit yourself to no more than two sets of sheets for each bed in your household: one to dress the bed with and a clean set to have at the ready. No extra just-in-case sheets clogging up your closets and drawers! I would also suggest limiting your bedding color palette for each room, so that the sheet sets can be mixed and matched in a pinch. That way, you can easily swap in the duvet cover from one set if there's an accidental spill or if you want a fresh pillowcase.

Lighting

Bedroom lighting is critical to creating a relaxing mood—don't let a lack of space make you compromise on a lighting design. Overhead lights can be placed on a dimmer, a simple upgrade you can do yourself or hire out to a handyman. For bedside lighting, you can save space on your nightstand with a wall-mounted sconce. Today it's possible to purchase a wide variety of attractive plug-in models—no electrician required. An even cheaper option is a clip lamp from a hardware store.

Bedside tables

Bedside tables are tricky to get right—especially in a small space. They're often too wide or too tall. But remember you don't need to buy something designed

to be a bedside table: you can place a small dresser, a low bookshelf, a desk, a stool, or a chair next to your bed, if it fits your space and needs. For extra-small spaces, look for wall-mounted options or even a simple shelf. However, don't be tempted to go without: it's nice to have a place to put a cup of water or your book.

Make your bed

Do this every single day. It's too big a part of your home not to! In a small space, especially any studio or one-room situation, an unmade bed is automatically going to make your whole home feel like a mess. If you're not a bed maker, give it a try. Commit to making your bed for one week and see how you feel. Once you start, I bet you'll wonder why you didn't do it all along. Need further convincing? A National Sleep Foundation poll found that survey participants who reported regularly making their bed were also more likely to say that they got a good night's sleep most nights than those who do not. A better looking home and better sleep? You'd be crazy not to make your bed.

cook & eat

I love to cook. I hail from a family of serious cooks who celebrate with food. My childhood home had a large kitchen with a center island, a breakfast table, and a six-burner commercial-grade stove. We had a pantry and a microwave the size of an oven, appliances for days, and a pot rack bursting with every shape and size of pan. It was a Martha Stewart–esque fantasy of a kitchen and it was great. But do you know what it wasn't? Necessary.

Great meals can be turned out in fifty square feet just as easily as they can be made in five hundred square feet. In fact, I might argue it's easier to cook in a smaller space where everything is close at hand. Having worked two summers for a catering company, I know that you can cook just about anything just about anywhere, with whatever you have on hand. I have prepared meals for fifty on two portable propane burners with the top of a cooler and a lobster trap as my only work surfaces.

I'm not alone in my belief that a small kitchen is not a barrier to fine cooking. Writing in the *New York Times*, where he was once a columnist, cookbook author Mark Bittman relayed a time when a journalist asked him what he considered essential in a modern kitchen. Bittman replied, "A stove, a sink, a refrigerator, some pots and pans, a knife, and some serving spoons. All else is optional."

If you're planning your small space from scratch, you have a lot of decisions to make, from appliances to counter materials. Don't rush. You're unlikely to renovate again, so it's important to get it right. If you're hoping to renovate an existing kitchen, take the time to observe how you use the space. Make a list of what you like and don't like about your existing kitchen. Observe which places always seem to end up a mess.

THE BIG SOLUTIONS

Dishwasher

Unless you eat out all the time, a dishwasher is an appliance that earns its place in even the smallest of homes. If you don't have the standard twenty-four inches to spare, an eighteen-inch dishwasher can do a day's worth of dishes for most families. Another small-space dishwashing solution is an under-the-sink unit like my family has (see page 150).

Refrigerator

Fridges have been getting bigger and bigger in recent years, but you can easily make do with a compact model. The advantages of a small fridge are many. You are much less likely to buy more food than you can eat

◁   When interior designer Emily Butler renovated the kitchen in her one-bedroom apartment in New York City, she opted for a petite 24-inch Bertazzoni stove to make room for counter space on either side of her sink. Custom cabinetry allowed Emily to make use of every inch, like the narrow space to the left of the range that holds baking sheets and cooling racks.

Our current twenty-four-inch stove is ample for any home cooking I do. A separate cooktop and wall oven can open up space-saving solutions, but these will be more expensive than a stand-alone or slide-in range. A two-burner cooktop is also an option, though not one I would recommend for avid cooks. In the most extreme cases, like inside a camper or a tiny house, a plug-in induction burner and a high-quality countertop toaster oven can replace traditional stoves. A microwave is one thing I think you can go without. You can reheat anything on the stovetop or in the oven.

Sink

A corner sink can take advantage of an often under-utilized area in the kitchen and simultaneously make room for a longer expanse of counter space elsewhere. A built-in drainboard is also a clever way to streamline your sink area. Instead of a clunky plastic tray taking up counter space, you have a built-in place to rest your drying rack or a few dishes.

Cabinets

Cabinets that go all the way to the ceiling greatly increase your cabinet space and eliminate the awkward above-the-cabinet area that usually collects dust. Use the high-up storage for items you use infrequently, such as vases, candlesticks, and specialized tools and appliances.

before it goes bad, and having a small fridge forces you to use up the condiments and other long-lasting items that can crowd a fridge. There are also lots of things that you don't need to store in the fridge. Many types of produce are happy left out on the counter, and there's no need to keep multiple bottles of wine or water chilled at one time.

Stove and Oven

With stoves and ovens, you have many options. I've cooked on all sizes of stoves, and I can confidently say that a twenty-inch model is just fine for most things (though not all baking sheets will fit inside these!).

Clockwise from top left: An 18-inch dishwasher, custom drawer dividers, kitchen cabinets that reach the ceiling, and a Corian counter with a built-in drainboard.

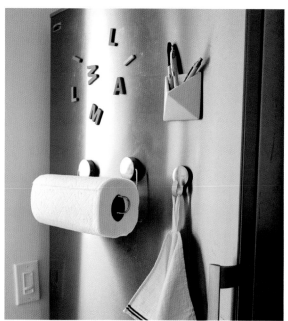

Clockwise from top left: An over-the-sink dish drainer, an over-the-stove cutting board,
a variety of magnetic fridge organizers, and a wall-mounted knife magnet.

THE LITTLE SOLUTIONS

An over-sink dish rack frees up the usual counter space a dish rack takes up. They only hold a few dishes, so keep a microfiber dish-drying mat tucked away for times when you have a large number of dishes to dry.

If you're pressed for counter space, an over-stovetop cutting board can give you a much-needed work surface (while you're not actively cooking, that is!).

A hanging fruit basket clears up counter space and lets your produce breathe.

A magnetic knife rack is more space efficient than a traditional knife block and is safer than keeping knives in a drawer with other utensils.

Clear your fridge of the usual paper clutter and put that space to work with magnetic organizers. These handy tools include paper towel holders, spice racks, and even knife racks.

A pegboard has been a classic way to make use of vertical space ever since Julia Child famously hung her *batterie de cuisine* from one in her Cambridge home.

Install a few cup hooks to the underside of your cabinets to create an easy-access coffee station and free up some cabinet space formerly used by your mugs.

If your cabinets don't reach the ceiling, add a few bins to the under-utilized space above. Use them to store items such as paper towels, foods from a wholesale club, rarely used appliances, and party supplies.

a not-quite minimalist kitchen checklist

1 paring knife
1 chef's knife
1 serrated knife
1 vegetable peeler
1 can opener
1 whisk
1 spatula
1 spring-loaded tongs
1 set measuring spoons
1 set measuring cups
1 2-cup liquid measuring cup
2 wooden spoons
1 rubber spatula
1 Microplane grater
2 cutting boards
2 half baking sheets (18 x 13 inches)
1 set of 3 nesting mixing bowls
9-inch diameter skillet
11-inch diameter skillet
Stock pot
6-quart Dutch oven
2-quart sauce pot
1 colander
Hand mixer
1 3- or 4-quart baking dish

bathe

In a recent housing report, 37 percent of new homes had three or more (!) full bathrooms. While a large spa-like master bathroom that you don't have to share with anyone is a lovely idea, it is a luxury. Luckily, you can have that same feeling of cleanliness and restoration in a tiny space—even one you share with your whole family.

The first step to making the most of a small bathroom is to pare back what is stored within. The majority of us have cabinets overflowing with skin, hair, and beauty products that we never or rarely use. Have an honest reckoning with yourself, your spouse, and your kids about what you really use and get rid of the rest. Unfortunately, used toiletries are very hard to donate. However, if you are in possession of unopened goods, your local homeless shelter will be thrilled to take them off your hands.

Once you've pared back, a few design tricks can make your space work to its maximum potential and still feel like a place of relaxation. Changing bigger things in a bathroom can often mean a costly remodel, but there are also opportunities to make improvements without breaking the bank or your tile.

THE BIG SOLUTIONS

Swap a small medicine cabinet for one that is the same width but much taller; this mini renovation requires minimal reframing and drywall repair. Your light fixture may need to move up to accommodate it, but this should be easy for a handyman to do.

Assess your sink. Often switching this one thing can make a world of difference. If the bathroom feels crowded, replacing a clunky vanity with a pedestal sink can give you some breathing room. Likewise, if you have a pedestal sink but are dying for storage, a swap to a vanity can solve your problems.

For a less intensive makeover, try skirting a sink with self-adhesive Velcro and fabric hemmed to your desired height. You can hide toilet paper, your plunger, and more behind the curtained area.

◁ While costly, a full-on bathroom renovation can pay off in lifestyle improvement. For example, architect Yaiza Armbruster used a host of small-space tricks in this New York City bathroom: She swapped a bathtub for a walk-in shower stall outfitted with a seamless glass enclosure. The two-tone tile gives the room a sense of architecture and interest, while a built-in shampoo box and a floating sink vanity offer stylish storage.

"Make your home as comfortable
and attractive as possible and
then get on with the living."

ALBERT HADLEY

If you're renovating, ask yourself if you need a bathtub. A shower enclosure will make a room feel more spacious than a tub of the same size. If you are really pressed for space, you can ask your architect or designer about designing the whole room as a wet room.

THE LITTLE SOLUTIONS

Mount a shelf above the bathroom door to eke out a bit of space for extra toilet paper or toiletries.

Suction and wall-mount storage aren't just for dorm rooms: many manufacturers produce high-quality stainless-steel organizers that can be installed without screws.

Our bathroom is tiny, and when we hang a shower curtain it feels downright claustrophobic. Someday we might invest in a glass shower door, but our solution for now is to use a clear, plastic shower curtain, which leaves the room feeling more open.

Use the back of your door for towel storage: mount hooks or, if you prefer, towel bars—just be sure to leave enough room for towels not to overlap.

A double-rod shower curtain offers you a place to dry towels or hang clothes while keeping your shower curtain pulled closed. Opt for one that screws into the wall or tile—not a tension mounted one that is likely to fall down under the weight.

Decanted toiletries may seem fussy, but the simple, matching containers will instantly elevate the look of your bathroom (hello, spa-like feeling!). If you don't want to decant, just peel the label off for a more stream-lined look.

Small acrylic shelf risers are a fantastic way to use every square inch inside your medicine cabinet. If your medicine cabinet is really lacking in shelves, you can purchase replacement shelves and support pegs/slips to fit your cabinet.

work

In 2017, approximately eight million Americans were working from home, and the numbers have been rising each year. Today's technology has rendered the trappings of a traditional office obsolete: with laptops, mobile phones, and document-scanning apps, you can work from almost anywhere.

Creating a dedicated physical home for your work is a smart idea—even if it's just a drawer or crate where you keep your work things. I am no stranger to the needs of a home office. My husband runs his business from our home, and I worked from home as a freelancer for many years myself. I know that a proper home office can help you be more organized, focused, and serious about your work. I also know that it can drive you crazy if it takes over the living room or invades the bedroom.

If at all possible, do not set up your work zone in your sleeping space. Having your work right next to where you sleep is not a recipe for good rest. If this is the only place that you can squeeze in a work area, then find a way to transition the space from office to rest space. Can your work things get tucked away in a drawer each night? Or could you place a curtain to close off the "work" area at night?

You might also consider renting an office outside of your home. I did this when my husband and I first moved in together, and it made our small one-bedroom workable for two freelancers.

THE BIG SOLUTIONS

A wall-mounted desk is a smart solution in a small room because it has no legs to infringe on your space (they are also often much smaller than traditional desks). A desk can often be built into a wall-mounted storage system like The Container Store's Elfa, IKEA's Svalnäs series, and the Vitsoe Universal Shelving System.

Desks with a fold-down design have the distinct advantage of letting you close the door on work at the end of the day (they're also great at hiding a mess). You can drill a hole in the back of antique models for cord control.

Many a resourceful small-space dweller has moved their "office" into a closet. To make the most of this setup, get a custom desktop cut to fit your closet exactly.

A corner desk provides a workspace in what is often an under-utilized part of a room. Because of the triangular shape, you'll have plenty of leg space without the need for a giant desk.

◁ This clever standing desk is hidden in a built-in cabinet in the living room of interior designer Emily Butler. The drawers hold her fabric samples, files, and office supplies. When the doors are shut the "office" disappears. The adjacent cabinet acts as a coat closet, a feature the apartment lacked.

THE LITTLE SOLUTIONS

A pack-away "office" is the ultimate small-space solution. Whether you tuck yours into a tote bag, a vintage suitcase, or a storage crate, your office can easily disappear when not in use.

Coordinate supplies so that your desk takes up less visual clutter in your home. Ditch the junky pencil cup with every pen you took home from a conference in favor of a small selection of your favorite writing utensils.

Digitize everything! Paper is the bane of office spaces. Get in the habit of signing up for paperless options for your bills, statements, and even reading, such as magazines and newspapers. Scan the documents that still come in a paper form and recycle the originals.

For those few papers you do need to keep, limit your paper storage. For most individuals and families, even a single filing cabinet is likely more document storage than you need. Instead, try a file box.

A compact wireless printer will cut down on cord clutter and takes up a fraction of the space that a traditional printer uses.

When it's time to buy a new computer, opt for a laptop instead of a bulky desktop or an old-school tower.

stock only what you need.

When people set up their home offices, they often run out to the office supply store and buy enough paper clips, folders, and sticky notes for an entire company. Yes, a case of paper is cheaper than buying by the single ream, but consider the space it will occupy in your home and how long it will take you to use it up.

Clockwise from top left: A pack-away home office; California decorator Crystal Palecek's pool shed-turned-office; the Vitsoe Universal Shelving System used to create a wall-mounted workspace.

play

Even when they are tiny, children (and their playthings) manage to take up a lot of space. Before our son was born, I read everything I could in books and on blogs about the intersection between parenting and minimalism, but nothing I read prepared me for the reality of the clutter tied to young children.

Our son still has many fewer toys than his same-age peers, but little by little, his collection has grown, and I can now understand how families end up with the insane amounts of playthings that you find in most homes. Toys creep in unexpectedly and, if you're not vigilant, they can quickly take up more room than you have allotted.

In my own not-quite-two-bedroom apartment, my husband and I have taken an unconventional approach: we gave our son the actual bedroom and took the smaller bedroom for ourselves. At this stage in his life, he needs room to play more than we need extra space to sleep. Some friends are surprised when they see our setup, but I would argue giving children the larger room can cut kid clutter out of the rest of the house, meaning you end up with more adult space overall. While parents of young kids are notoriously pressed for time, it is worth the effort to think and plan ways to tackle the toys.

THE BIG SOLUTIONS

Look for storage pieces that can grow with your child. Avoid anything too specifically "baby" in style or function. Opt for bookcases with shelves that can be moved to different heights for maximum flexibility.

A dedicated playroom is rare in a small space, so children's play areas must fit into their sleeping space or the family's living area. Seek out playthings that match your décor. When making purchases for your child, ask yourself, "Do I like this? Would I choose this for myself? Will my child like this in five years? In ten?"

Think long and hard about large toys. Play kitchens, doll-houses, and toy garages all take up a lot of space. Before buying one of these behemoths, consider if your child can enjoy this kind of play elsewhere, like at daycare or Sunday school. There might also be a smaller version that will bring as much joy. For example, instead of a space-hogging play kitchen, our son has a scaled-down version that fits on a shelf.

Look for playthings that fold up or pack flat. Some play tents and tunnels fold down to almost nothing. A play mat printed with a road scene can be rolled up (while a toy car ramp cannot).

◁   If you have to see it every day, make it something you love. This bentwood child's table and chairs blend into the living room's décor more readily than a brightly colored plastic set would.

Wait and see. The special play gym or the beautiful toy tent that seem so needed now might just be a passing phase or desire. Wait at least a month before buying anything for your child that takes up major real estate.

THE LITTLE SOLUTIONS

Take a look at your child's preschool: I bet everything is in a labeled basket or clear box, or sits directly on a shelf. Try this at home to prompt your child, babysitter, or grandparent to put things back in their places.

Avoid the classic toy box. I have never once seen a toy box being used as an efficient way to store playthings. Instead, you open them up to find a wasteland of disorganized toys.

Catalogs are filled with all manner of cute storage bins, but beware: most bins are too big! Like toy boxes, the problem with big bins is that it's hard to find a toy within, and when they inevitably get dumped out, they create a huge mess. Choose a greater number of small bins.

Under-the-bed storage is a good way to store toys that are not played with every day. A bed with built-in drawers is great, but you can also use simple crates. Place felt furniture pads or small casters underneath to cut down on the scraping sound from pulling them across wood floors.

Wall-mounted toy and book storage is a space-saver and can double as wall art.

dealing with toy clutter

1. If it's broken and can't be fixed, toss or recycle it. Throw away or recycle any junky toys that have come home from birthday parties or the doctor's office.

2. When purging, ask your child which toys feel "babyish." Feeling like a big boy or big girl is often a good motivator to part with outgrown playthings.

3. Listen to your child. If you ask him which toys to get rid of and he suggests something expensive or gifted by a friend, don't resist his desire to let it go.

4. Cull a selection of less-played-with toys to go live at a relative's house. Toys get imbued with new life when they've been out of sight for a period.

5. When your child is not at home, gather up the toys you know she hasn't played with in a long time. Put them into a box in a remote spot. If she asks for a toy, you can retrieve it, but anything that goes unrequested for six months can be donated.

6. Read books with your kids about the value of decluttering like *Too Many Toys* by David Shannon, *The Berenstain Bears Think of Those In Need*, and *Kiki & Jax* by Marie Kondo.

7. Ask friends and family members to give your children experiences, books, food treats, and clothing—not more toys.

8. Try to stick to a one in, one out policy. If a visiting relative brings a new stuffed animal, find an old one to recycle. If you buy a new puzzle, donate one to your church's daycare.

Clockwise from top left: Under-the-bed toy storage, children's books on wall-mounted book ledges, a simple bookshelf with adjustable shelves, and a mini version of the often hulking play kitchen.

store

Closets, basements, and attics are a boon to any small space, but so often they can become dumping grounds for clutter and things we don't actively use. Getting control of your storage space takes time and effort, but once you've organized so that everything has a place, your home will feel larger, I promise.

THE BIG SOLUTIONS

Closet Systems

In my first studio apartment I had a luxurious amount of closet space, courtesy of the previous tenant who had gone through the trouble of moving the apartment's front door to make room for a larger clothing closet. However, she'd stopped there. Inside there was just a single hanging rod and one shelf. Wanting to make the most of my storage space, I called up a consultant from California Closets and outfitted the space with shelves and drawers customized for my needs. Since then, I've been telling everyone I know that it was the best money I have ever spent on my home, and it's true!

My architect friend tsk-tsks my enthusiasm for custom-designed closet systems as overpriced, but she's coming from the point of view of an expert who has a Rolodex of cabinet makers at her disposal, and she likely doesn't see what a mess her clients' closets become after a few months of living in their homes. Part of what you pay for with a custom closet service is the expertise of someone who has designed dozens if not hundreds of closets before, and you don't have to spend the money on a contractor or architect to plan, demo, and install the new fittings into the space.

If custom is out of reach, I have also outfitted a closet myself with the Elfa system from The Container Store. How well a DIY service will work for you will depend entirely on the space you have. For example, with set shelf sizes you may end up with big gaps that must go unused. On the plus side, the systems could not be easier to install.

THE LITTLE SOLUTIONS

In a tight space, consider replacing your closet door with a set of heavyweight curtains: you'll free up the floor space the door would have needed to swing, which may enable a new furniture arrangement or a smoother passage.

You can also replace traditional doors with a sliding barn door or, if budget allows, a pocket door that recedes into the nearby wall.

◁ A few well-chosen accessories and matching hangers go a long way toward making your closet feel more organized, but the only way to truly keep this space tidy is not to store more in a closet than it can comfortably hold.

If you keep your traditional door, put it to work: a closet door is an ideal vertical space to store any number of things or to mount a full-length mirror.

Steal this trick from professional organizers: invest in matching, high-quality hangers to make your closet *feel* more orderly. If you opt for the velvet flocked ones, they'll let you squeeze in a few more garments.

Install a few small screw-in hooks on the bare wall inside your closet to hang jewelry and accessories.

If paring down your wardrobe is a struggle, try this: pack all the clothes you don't love into your suitcases. If after a few months you haven't missed those items, you'll likely feel ready to donate or sell them.

Thinking beyond the merely utilitarian, making a closet into a jewel box of color or pattern with paint or wallpaper is an excellent way to add personality and surprise without visually overwhelming the rest of your small space.

test-drive tiny

Anecdotes abound about families or empty nesters who have downsized their space and reaped the benefits of their newfound freedom. Yet many of us hesitate to make the leap ourselves. We think, "But what if it's too small?" If you're considering a downsize, try these strategies to figure out how small is right for you.

Go slow. Overnight change is not possible (or even desirable) when we're talking about downsizing a lifetime of stuff. If your goal is to move into a smaller space, start with the decluttering and de-owning process (see page 161 for tips). Once you start to feel the lightness that comes with fewer possessions, you may feel more confident about moving forward.

Give yourself a false sense of small. Close the doors to the guest bedrooms, the attic, the formal dining or living room, and any other infrequently used rooms. Note how long you go before entering these spaces and what causes you to enter when you do. You may discover it'd be cheaper to pay for guests' hotel rooms twice a year than to maintain a larger home, or that your attic or basement is only housing the things you no longer want or need.

Be an anthropologist. Observe your friends and family who are living in smaller homes than you. Read books and magazines about small spaces. Try to glean what might work (and what won't work) for you. Perhaps you can forgo a formal dining room or maybe you'd be just fine with a teeny-tiny bedroom.

Test-drive tiny. Before taking the leap to a smaller space, give it a try beforehand. Spend your next vacation in a rental house instead of a hotel to give a small space a trial run. Consider renting out your own home while you rent a smaller space (ideally, pocketing a profit), if you're still unsure.

Plan, plan, plan, and plan some more. If you're ready to make the move and have a new home in mind, take the time to figure out how you'll live in your new space. Sketch out floor plans and measure to see how your current life will fit into your new home. Testing out your new space on paper will save you time and money and will help you make the smartest choices.

Pack away your "collections" and your "maybes." When I moved into an apartment in Brooklyn, I knew I wanted to tear out a closet and put in wall-mounted bookshelves, but it took me two years to get around to it. During that time, my books sat in boxes. When I realized my books had gone unread for two years, I was able to seriously cut back on my collection, donating more than half. Start by boxing up the collections you aren't actively using and the things you are hesitant to get rid of now. After a couple months in storage, you may feel the confidence to finally let them go.

committing to tiny

Part of the secret to living small is to anticipate and adapt to life changes. When planning your space, try to look ahead. Imagine any future changes that you may need to account for today; for example, where do you see your family in five years or in ten? Asking these questions will help you make decisions when you move, renovate, or even purchase an investment piece of furniture—and making smart choices can help you stay in your small space longer.

WHEN THINGS GET TIGHT

What do you do when your small space suddenly feels a little *too* small? First, assess what's going on. For example, if it's winter, perhaps your space feels small because you're home and indoors more than usual. In that case, make it a point to get out and explore.

If you have recently started sharing your space, it is sure to feel cramped. My old one-bedroom felt practically claustrophobic when my then-boyfriend, now-husband, moved in. It took a few months for us to ease into cohabitation. The secret here is to make sure you get some time alone at home: kick your partner out one night a week, so you can putter solo like you did before deciding to shack up.

Children also have a way of making a home seem too tiny. New parents feel their home is overrun with baby gear and others find themselves wishing for a third bedroom when a second baby arrives. Again, these seasons are relatively short: the bouncy seat and stroller will be gone before you know it. In just a few months, your baby will (hopefully) sleep through the night and can begin sharing a room with your big kid.

When a friend's daughter turned fifteen, she no longer wanted to share a room with her brother. My friend was seriously debating selling her much-loved apartment when I suggested she consider remodeling instead. My pal and her husband invested in a custom-made loft bed for their kids' shared room, closet systems for all the closets, and a down-to-the-studs bathroom remodel that made the sole bath space feel more spacious. The work was expensive, but even the cost of more than twenty thousand dollars was nothing in comparison to what she'd spend on the expenses associated with moving (not to mention buying a larger apartment). Plus, many of the upgrades on her bucket list added value to her home in the long run. The

remodel was also inconvenient, but it was temporary. Once the family settled back in, they felt like they had a new home, one that was better suited to their needs.

Remember the long view. Life's stages come and go, sometimes quickly and sometimes ever so slowly. If your space has begun to feel too small, take a step back and examine what's happening now. Don't let today's temporary discomfort force you into moving into a space that's bigger than you really need.

THE WORLD OUTSIDE YOUR HOME

One of the secrets to living small is what's outside your door. Anyone can go a little stir-crazy cooped up in a tiny spot, day in and day out. Getting out of the house is the cure to cabin fever, and it can take many forms, from a daily ritual to a once-a-year vacation.

Use public spaces. The library, the park, the local playground, or your neighborhood coffee shop—these are all places you can escape to when you need a little breathing room. When my husband and I were in the early, sleep-deprived days of parenting, we'd take turns taking our noisy toddler out to a diner or coffee shop in the morning, so the other parent could get some shut eye. We always visit the library on rainy days when that antsy inside feeling is likeliest to set in, and we plan playdates at the playground on days when we can't handle the chaos in our tiny home.

Rent selectively. When my husband first moved into my apartment, I leased a desk in a coworking space instead of working at home. It was an added expense, but much less than the cost of the two apartments we'd had previously, and less than the cost of a larger rental we might share. I have a musician friend who took a

storage space is not the answer

Americans are addicted to storage. According to the Self Storage Association, 1 in 11 Americans has self-storage, and if you added up all the storage facilities in the US, they would measure 82.5 square miles (approximately the size of Las Vegas).

While storing your things off-site might seem like a great way to make your small space work, it is avoiding the real problem (that you have too much stuff) and costing you more than you likely realize. Even though I hate the idea of self-storage, I briefly had a unit myself, and my experience tells you a lot about the problem of self-storage.

When my husband and I went to sell our apartment, our real estate broker advised us that our place was too cluttered and suggested we get a storage space for a few months while we staged our apartment for sale. We knew she was right (we wanted to move because we felt we'd outgrown the space). We paid a premium for a storage unit close to our home because we figured it would be worth it to be able to readily access our things.

After a full day of decluttering and moving things to the storage unit, we proudly showed our broker the results of our efforts. She was unimpressed and encouraged us to keep going. After another weekend of moving out everything we could imagine not needing every day our broker was satisfied. A funny thing happened along the way: suddenly our cramped apartment felt airy and light. Our place looked great—and it was so much easier to clean!

We ended up having that storage space for six months. In that time, we never once needed anything from the unit. There was one occasion when I wished I had my sewing machine to hem something, but I just took it to the dry cleaner and paid a few dollars to have their tailor do it. When we were finally ready to move into our new apartment, we confronted the storage unit. Looking in at the sea of boxes, we couldn't even recall what was inside. How could we have a 6' x 6' room full of things we couldn't remember?

If you already have a self-storage unit, tackle this before you start in on your home. Think of it as a debt that needs to be paid off first before you can start saving for your dream house/vacation/education. Address the issue head on rather than continuing to pay rent on your space every month.

If you're thinking of renting storage to make your small space work, don't do it. The costs are likely to add up to more than the value of the things you plan to store. Instead, do the hard work of sorting through your things, paring back, and living within your allotted space.

lease on a recording studio and then sublet it to other musicians when he wasn't using it; not only was this option less expensive than getting a bigger apartment, it actually ended up being an extra source of income. I know a dad who rented shower space in a roundabout way when he opted for a fancier gym membership so he could exercise and shower at the gym rather than fight with the rest of his family for bathroom time in a one-bath apartment.

Party elsewhere. When it comes time to hosting a big event, host the party somewhere else. Alison Mazurek, author of the blog *600 Sq Ft and a Baby,* refers to this as "outsourcing" space. Yes, hosting in a venue or a restaurant will cost more than having a party at home, but a few hundred dollars a couple times a year is nothing compared to the larger rent or mortgage payment you'd be making on a home large enough to host big celebrations.

Leverage outdoor areas. Look at your outdoor areas with a critical eye: you may find hidden space here. A patio can go from a single season dining area to a three season one with the addition of an outdoor space heater. In warmer climates, adding an outdoor shower can make a single-bathroom house bearable for a large family. Blogger Whitney Morris of the *Tiny Canal Cottage* went so far as to convert an outdoor shed into overflow clothing storage at her Los Angeles home. There are many ways to co-opt your outdoor space to make your indoor space more livable.

IGNORE OTHERS' EXPECTATIONS

As you embrace living small, your friends and family may not support you in your journey. The American dream has been about bigger and better for so long that, as a society, we've lost sight of what is enough. In 1951 the average size of a new home was 874 square feet. In 2015, at the peak of new building sizes, that number was 2,740—that's nearly three times as large! We've been brought up to believe that we need (and deserve) an obscene amount of space.

My own family seemed perplexed when my husband and I opted to buy a 690-square-foot one-bedroom apartment (to be converted to two) for our soon-to-be family of three. My mother even encouraged me to "stretch" our budget to get a "real" two bedroom. But those extra costs didn't make sense to us. We were looking to save nearly $175,000 up front by opting for the smaller apartment, but we'd still have two bedrooms, a kitchen, a living room, and an ample vestibule. Choosing the bigger apartment would have meant a larger mortgage payment, bigger utility bills, and more to clean.

But the world is different now: the sunny outlook of American prosperity of the latter part of the twentieth century has dimmed. We have seen the promise that real estate will always go up in value as a hollow one. We've watched our fellow citizens rack up debt and fail to save for their futures. We now know the threats of climate crisis are real and pressing. To be mindful and conscious with our choice to live small is more important now than ever before.

When your relatives frown at your small place or even make you feel like you've failed somehow, patiently explain *why* you choose to live small—and then leave it there. Live your life by the ideals that you hold dear. Make an example of living small, persuade through your actions, through your contentment, through your freedom.

CELEBRATING SMALL

You've chosen to live small—hurray for you! You've figured out how to make your small space work. Using the ideas in the chapters of this book, you've tweaked, styled, and organized your home to fit your lifestyle. You've applied your ethos of living with less space to living with less all around: less clutter, fewer social obligations, a streamlined wardrobe, and maybe you've even embraced the shared economy.

There's one more step to fully living small: invite someone else in.

Just because your home is tiny is no excuse not to invite friends, family, and even brand-new acquaintances into your home. A home truly comes alive when it's full of laughter and life—and by sharing your small space, you may just inspire someone else toward a path to living small.

When I lived in my 225-square-foot studio, I didn't have a dining table but that didn't stop me from having dinner parties: I'd lay out the meal on the coffee table and pull my two chairs up opposite the sofa. Each of those crowded, plates-on-knees meals is a memory I cherish. When I hosted a larger party during the holidays, I used my fire escape as overflow fridge space and filled the bathtub with ice to chill the party drinks.

My friend Vanessa and her husband live in a tiny one-bedroom, but Vanessa hosts our book club just as often as our other friends with more spacious pads. When we come to Vanessa's home, half of us sit on the floor, the rest of us curl up together on her L-shaped sofa—and it's great. Trust me when I tell you that no one will judge your small space, and no one will mind being a little crowded in. In fact, they may even enjoy it more than a party in a big house, where guests are too spread out for conversations to pop up naturally.

Ask someone over or host a gathering. You'll get that good energy from other people and also from your own, better self that you tend to be when you entertain. Fill your small space with life.

BIG GRATITUDE

I want to close this book by encouraging you to take a moment of thanks for your home—wherever it is, however large or small it may be. Sometimes in the hustle and bustle of our everyday lives, we forget just how fortunate we are—even in the hard or low-down times. To have a roof over your head is so much more than millions of people have today.

Include your home in your thoughts of gratitude; occasionally save a place for it in your prayers. We remember to pause and be thankful for our health and our prosperity. But when was the last time you meditated on the good fortune of your home? Look past your punch list of projects and your dreams of a picture-perfect space and say thank you for the home you have.

"The home should be the treasure chest of living."

LE CORBUSIER

further reading

Apartment Therapy's Big Book of Small, Cool Spaces, by Maxwell Ryan

Home Comforts: The Art and Science of Keeping House, by Cheryl Mendelson

How to Live in Small Spaces: Design, Furnishing, Decoration, Detail for the Smaller Home, by Terence Conran

Remodelista: The Organized Home: Simple, Stylish Storage Ideas for All Over the House, by Julie Carlson and Margot Guralnick

Simple Matters: Living with Less and Ending Up with More, by Erin Boyle

Simplicity Parenting: Using the Extraordinary Power of Less to Raise Calmer, Happier, and More Secure Kids, by Kim John Payne

Small Space Style: Because You Don't Need to Live Large to Live Beautifully, by Whitney Leigh Morris

The Life-Changing Magic of Tidying Up: The Japanese Art of Decluttering and Organizing, by Marie Kondo

The Little Book of Tidying: Declutter Your Home and Your Life, by Beth Penn

The New American Dream: Living Well in Small Homes, by James Gauer

The Not So Big House: A Blueprint for the Way We Really Live, by Sarah Susanka

The Real Simple Method to Organizing Every Room: And How To Keep It That Way, by The Editors of Real Simple

The Simplicity Reader, by Elaine St. James

Zero Waste Home: The Ultimate Guide to Simplifying Your Life by Reducing Your Waste, by Bea Johnson

resources

Bredabeds

Bredabeds sells the Murphy beds it manufactures directly to consumers, thereby offering prices close to wholesale rates. In addition to traditional Murphy beds, Bredabeds offers horizontally-oriented wall beds.
bredabeds.com

California Closets

The name in custom closet solutions, California Closets also offers Murphy beds and office build-outs. With 120+ showrooms in the US, the company has designers in most areas.
californiaclosets.com

Chairish

An online marketplace for vintage furniture, art, and décor, Chairish's offerings are curated, so there's less junk to wade through.
chairish.com

Chasing Paper

This manufacturer of temporary wallpaper is known for its designer collaborations and high-quality papers. Their peel-and-stick adhesive makes their wallpapers a great solution for renters.
Chasingpaper.com

eBay

The original online auction site, eBay is still a great place to source secondhand furnishings and other housewares. Limit your search by "Item Location" to find the pieces that are closest to home.
eBay.com

Elfa

Owned by the Container Store, Elfa is a wall-hung closet and organization system that you can customize to your space and install yourself.
containerstore.com/elfa

Etsy

More than just a marketplace for handmade goods, Etsy is also a major shopping site for vintage and custom furniture and home accessories.
Etsy.com

Fagor

This Spanish appliance company makes compact appliances that are much smaller than many domestically made models.

FLOR

This company's modular carpet tiles help you create a custom rug to fit any space. And because they

are movable, you can use them in future spaces by reconfiguring or adding on to your original tiles.
flor.com

Gothic Cabinet Craft

Based in New York, Gothic Cabinet Craft has been making "real wood furniture" since 1969. The company's signature storage beds come with a lifetime guarantee.
gothiccabinetcraft.com

Habitat ReStore

These stores and donation centers are independently operated by local branches of Habitat for Humanity. They sell and accept donations of new and gently used furniture, appliances, home goods, building materials, and more.
habitat.org/restores

IKEA

Famously affordable, the Swedish retailer is a source for furniture, wardrobes, and closet systems. When purchasing IKEA furniture, opt for pieces made from solid wood, glass, and metal, and avoid those made from particleboard and other composite materials.
ikea.com

Muji

The minimalist Japanese lifestyle brand offers more than 7,000 items from soap to rice cookers, all of which are designed in a sophisticated and simple style. Many of its goods are compact in size, including its furniture, small appliances, and kitchen tools.
muji.com

Rejuvenation

A go-to shopping destination for hardware, lighting, fixtures, and a limited selection of antiques. Rejuvenation also sells home goods like furniture, bedding, baskets, and rugs with a focus on timeless style and natural material like wood, metal, and wool.
Rejuvenation.com

Resource Furniture

The Ferrari of wall beds, Resource Furniture's custom beds are made in Italy and flat-packed for shipment. The company has eighteen showrooms in the US where they also sell all manner of "transforming furniture," including coffee tables that rise to meal height, dinner tables that expand to seat ten, and stackable dining chairs.
resourcefurniture.com

Schoolhouse

A source for all types of lighting, including space-saving wall sconces, Schoolhouse is also a resource for hardware, such as hooks, knobs, and other utility items that have a timeless design and sturdy construction.
schoolhouse.com

Shaker Workshops

This company offers old-school Shaker-style pegs rails, which can be custom ordered in any length.
shakerworkshops.com

Simple Wood Goods

This Ohio-based company makes what its name suggests: Simple wood furnishings designed by an architect-turned-maker.
simplewoodgoods.com

Smeg

This Italian appliance manufacturer pairs high design with the latest energy-saving technology to produce appliances that fit well in small kitchens, including twenty-four-inch ranges and counter-depth retro-style fridges.
smeg.com

The Container Store

This is a one-stop shop for your organization needs including boxes, baskets, and bins. Just steer clear of the many plastic options for a homier, more natural look of paper, wood, metal, and glass.
containerstore.com

Vitsoe

The longtime manufacturer for the 606 Universal Shelving System designed by Dieter Rams, which can be customized to fit any space.
vitsoe.com

West Elm

If you're looking for affordable to mid-range furniture that's sized right for small spaces, West Elm delivers with small-scale sofas, petite desks, and more.
westelm.com

Yamazaki

A great resource for attractive home organizers, especially their magnetic kitchen options, this Japanese company's wares can be found on Amazon and through specialty retailers.

featured architects, builders, and designers

Hemsath Construction (builder), pages 104–117
Los Angeles, CA
(818) 219-3969
Alan Hemsath

Atelier Armbruster (architect), pages 5 and 186
New York, NY
atelierarmbruster.com
Yaiza Armbruster
Natalia Lorca Ruiz

Emily C. Butler (interior designer), pages 180 and 190
New York, NY
emilycbutler.com

Glenn Ban Interiors, pages 70–81
East Hampton, NY
glennban.com

Kenny A. D. Payero (architect), pages 10–21
New York, NY
kennypayero.com

Mark Enos (decorator) pages 10–21
New York

Rocky Mountain Tiny Houses, pages 94–103
Durango, CO
rockymountaintinyhouses.com
Greg Parham

Shira Gill, pages 132–143 and 160
Berkley, CA
shiragill.com

Shavonda Gardner, pages 118–131
Sacramento, CA
Sgstyleblog.com

Open Haus Design, pages 104–117
Venice Beach, CA
openhausdesign.com
Claudia Wiehen
Cynthia Salah Kraus

acknowledgments

Thank you to Weston, my partner in life, and now my partner in this book. I am so grateful for the wonderful photos and the enthusiasm with which they were produced: we sure had some fun. Thank you also for giving me the time and space to write these words. There is no one I would rather live small with than you.

So many thanks are due to our parents, who all took turns watching our son while this book was being made. We are grateful for your support and for raising us to want better not more.

This book would not have come to be without all the individuals and families who opened their doors to us: this book is yours as much as it is ours. Thank you for your generosity and the inspiration. Thank you also to the many more who sent photos of their homes in the early stages of production; we wish we had enough pages to feature them all.

Sharon Bowers, I am so grateful you believed in this book and me when I had little more than a few pages of an idea.

Thank you to Katie Killebrew and everyone at Gibbs Smith for bringing this book to life. I am so grateful for the chance to publish this book with such a creative and understanding team.

Finally, a special thanks to our son, William: the light you bring to our life is essential for everything we do.

ABOUT THE AUTHORS

Longtime residents of New York City, Laura Fenton and Weston Wells live in Jackson Heights, Queens, with their son, William. Laura is a writer and editor, who has held staff positions at the magazines *Budget Living, Good Housekeeping,* and *Parents*; her writing has also been published in *Better Homes & Gardens, Country Living, Curbed.com,* and *New York* magazine. Weston is a photographer, whose work has been published in *Monocle, Esquire, Condé Nast Traveler, Departures,* and *Variety*. The couple has previously collaborated on projects for *Wilder Quarterly* and *Kinfolk*. You can follow them on Instagram by following Laura at @littlehousenyc and Weston at @weston.wells.